The Joy of Giving

THE *Joy* OF GIVING

b y

BEN GILL

MYRIAD COMMUNICATIONS, INC.

Library of Congress Catalog Card Number:94-77171
Gill, Ben
  The Joy of Giving.
ISBN 0-9642146-0-1

▲ ▲ ▲
DEDICATION
▼ ▼ ▼

This book is dedicated to those people who have come
to know the joy of giving and in doing so have made
life a victorious pilgrimage.

ACKNOWLEDGEMENT

Over the years, I have come to appreciate more and more the model of generosity set for me by my mother. My father passed away when I was less than a year old, and my mother, with two young sons, set out to make a life for us. She tilled the soil of an Arkansas farm to scratch out a living. When I became ill with asthma, she moved us to New Mexico and worked for the Atomic Laboratory at Los Alamos.

Through all of this, she taught us to give. We went to church and we were expected to put our nickel or dime in the offering envelope. But the lessons also carried over into the world around us. No one in need was ever turned away from our door. Giving was a way of life in the Gill household. I thank her for setting that example in the joy of giving.

There have been others who have influenced the lessons of this manuscript. My friend and business partner, Bill Wilson, has taught me that giving is a learned experience, and that the challenge of our job is not to raise money, but rather to teach people to give. Now after having raised almost $3 billion for the cause of the Kingdom, I thank him for holding to that principle rather than taking the shortcut to just hustle the crowd.

Then there are the people with whom I have worked over the years. Many of them are portrayed within the pages of this book. Oh, how much I have learned from them. Every day, I witness people—not always spiritual giants, but simple people—who go about their lives with a spirit of generosity that is refreshing and often profound. I have learned from them, and from those lessons come the words that are published here.

To my daughter, Dee Gill, a reporter for *The Wall Street Journal* in London, who edited my first draft and encouraged me to try again.

And, finally, to my fellow staff members at Resource Services, Inc. (RSI) who read the manuscript and critiqued the message. To my assistant, Patricia Hail, who corrected my spelling and put everything in the right place. To all of those who have taken this work and helped it become a reality, I express my thanks.

▲ ▲ ▲

TABLE OF CONTENTS

▼ ▼ ▼

CHAPTER I

THE PROCESS BEGINS

M y life has been spent helping people learn the gift of giving. After twenty-five years in this pursuit, I come now to tell you that one fact has become increasingly clear: the happiest people on earth are the people who have learned the joy of giving.

I say that after having seen it experienced by thousands of people in thousands of ways. I saw it in the face of an elderly woman in Dallas who had just decided to take a Saturday job in order to be able to give five dollars per week to the building program of her church. The tremendous joy of that decision was evident in her eyes as she told of her decision.

I heard it in the voice of a businessman in Atlanta who had made a commitment to give a million dollars to help build a new sanctuary for his church. He later told me that nothing he had ever done in his life had meant as much to him as that decision to stretch himself in the giving process.

I felt the emotions of the moment when a young couple in North Carolina decided to give up their dream home to help build a new church. There was something deeply moving when they shared with me that they had a lifetime to build their home, but might never again have the opportunity to build God's house. Somehow, they did not want to miss that opportunity.

Over the years, I have seen the experience worked out in a multitude of ways, but in every case there has been one common denominator. In all those years and in all of those experiences, I have never once heard anyone say they regretted their sacrifice. In fact, to the contrary, most have said they wished they had come to know the joy of giving long before they did. Again, I say, it has been my experience that the happiest people on earth are the people who know how to give.

For most of us, the opportunities to give are many. Whether from the TV evangelist or the local minister, we are asked time and time again to give of our resources to meet a multitude of needs. As discerning donors, what are the factors that should influence our giving decisions?

Within the framework of personal confession, let me suggest a few. It has been my experience that for me to know the true joy of giving, I must be properly motivated. In fact, it is not an overstatement to say that giving, to be a joyous experience, must always begin with the proper motivation.

Personally, I was raised on the theology that you give or God "gets you." I remember, as a ten-year-old boy coming home from school one day, hearing that our neighbor's house had burned to the ground. That night, as my mother told my stepfather about it, she said, "Well, I knew something would happen. You know Henry stopped tithing last year." The lesson for the day was, "You give or God gets you!" That will scare you to death when you are ten years old!

I continued to be influenced by that approach while I attended the largest Baptist university in the world to prepare for the ministry. In four years of undergraduate work, no one ever challenged that ingrained theology of giving. From the university, I went to the largest Baptist seminary in the world for three years of graduate study. In all of my time there, no one ever challenged that theology of giving. I firmly believed that the proper motivation to give was a fear of the results if you did not give.

Finally, I am sent out into the world to pastor my first church and I preach a message of giving that is designed to scare people into "loving" sacrifice. And as a young pastor, I saw them give, but never once did I see anyone really happy about it. On Commitment Sunday when we took pledges for the budget, we always oversubscribed, but there was a gloominess about it. There was no joy.

I remember going to the Texas Baptist Evangelism Conference one year and hearing a sermon by Dr. S. M. Lockridge entitled "The Lordship of Christ." I remember so well when this great preacher said, "The God who owns the cattle upon a thousand hills just plain don't need your money. But aren't you glad that He has given you the opportunity to be a part of what He is doing."

Suddenly the light came on! Giving did not need to be coerced. Giving could be the joining in a partnership with God to do His will around the world. We could literally join hands with the Father to accomplish His divine purpose.

I could not wait to get back to my church. Immediately, I started preaching a new message about giving. And almost instantaneously, I saw a new response from the people. The next year when we pledged our budget, there was an excitement about it. People left the service that morning saying, "Pastor, I'm not sure how we are going to do what we pledged, but we are going to try. We just want to be a vital part of what our church is doing."

Giving—joyous giving—always begins with the proper motivation. I know that it is often popular to challenge people to give in order to receive God's blessings. This is the concept that you give and God gives back to you tenfold. That may be the result of giving, but it must not be the motivation for giving. I have seen people who gave generously and who, in a matter of months, endured great trial and hardship. Surely, one would not negate their generosities.

A few years ago, I sat with a man on a college campus in Virginia and looked up at a building that had his name on it. He told me how, a few years before, he had given the money for the building and how, to his surprise, the college had named the building for him. As we stood there that day, he said, "You know, two years after I gave the money for that building, my business went belly-up. Mark this down," he said. "I lost it all. But I have never regretted giving away money when I had it. In fact, to a great extent, the only thing that I have left is that which I gave away."

I have seen that experience repeated too many times to be comfortable with the concept that you give and God will always give back to you in kind.

Another motivation often applied is that of legalism. It is similar to the "give or God gets you" concept, but different in that those who would motivate through legalism expect you to give and be happy about it simply because "the Bible says you should be." In other words, it's the law. It's like the mother who says to her child, "You are going to eat that cabbage and you are going to like it!"

I have never seen people give joyously through legalistic motivation. Invariably, the people who give from this standpoint are the people who get in debates about whether or not you should tithe on "net or gross income." How gross!

When my friend, Douglas Farmer, was ordained to the ministry, he was sixteen years old and living in a little country town in Arkansas. I remember in the interrogation time how the council questioned him. I also remember the comments made by Bro. Henry Appleton. In a timbre that echoed the depth of death itself, he admonished the new minister. "Bro. Doug," he said, "before I lay my hands on you, I want to know if you will agree that from this day forth you will keep a little record of every dime, yea—even every cent that God may give you, and you will, on the first day of every week, return unto God that which is rightfully His?"

I listened as my friend looked into the end of that pointed finger and promised to do exactly that. Of course, I could just see poor Doug missing the gates of heaven because, somewhere in life, he failed to record the two-dollar birthday gift from Aunt Suzie.

Now before you brand me a heretic, I want you to know that I do believe there is an admonishment to return unto God a tithe—a response, if you please, to God's goodness in one's life. What I am saying is that fear and legalism are shallow motivations for that response.

Consider this for a moment: what would happen if, in the giving process, we chose not to operate from any of the standards mentioned thus far, but simply approached giving from the standpoint of walking in God's will? What could happen if the next time we had to make a giving decision, we simply asked, "Lord, what would You do through me in this giving opportunity?" What if the next time we were faced with a giving opportunity, we simply reaffirmed, "My motivation to respond in this situation is to express God's love through me toward this need."

What if we experimented with the concept that love and caring as God loves and cares could be our source of happiness? What if, rather than fear or legalism or any other lesser motivation, what if "God's will through me" became the standard by which we made our giving decisions?

During the twenty-five years of my stewardship ministry, I have helped raise money for a multitude of projects. Some churches were relocating their entire facilities, while others were paying off old and burdensome debts. One was raising money for water wells in Africa and another was building a bowling center for its recreation ministry.

In every case, no matter what the project, I have attempted to set forth a very simple goal. I have attempted to lead the people to be willing to say that the primary objective, the primary goal, is merely for every family in the church to determine God's will about their financial response to this particular need. Oh, we have built highly developed organizations to provide a framework for response, but the goal has always been to lead the people to seek and find the mind of God regarding their response.

That sounds easy, but believe me, it is often difficult. Perhaps it is more difficult for me, as a fund-raising consultant, than it is for the church. The difficulty for me is not that I do not believe this is the proper approach. The difficulty is in being faithful to the approach when given the opportunity for a "quick fix" that could produce a lot of money.

Let me give you an example. A few years ago, I was working with a church in south Florida where the financial need was greater than normal for the size of the church. We realized that sizeable gifts would be needed to reach the goal. In fact, we were specifically looking for a $500,000 gift. As we moved through the program, I noticed the Steering Committee Chairman was going through a great struggle with the decision about his commitment. One night after a meeting, we went out for a cup of coffee, and in that casual setting he began to talk freely about his struggle toward decision.

"Ben," he confessed, "never in my life have I labored with a decision more than this decision about my gift to this program. I know that you have seen others go through this same process. I really need your counsel. What do you think I should give?"

At that moment, I realized I had the opportunity and the ability to secure the $500,000 gift. The man sitting across the table from me had the financial resources to make that gift. He had specifically asked for my advice. What a perfect setup! The only problem was that, from the beginning, my challenge to him and to others in the church was simply to seek, find, and do the will of God. Falling back on that, I made my response.

"I know you asked me that question out of a sincere desire to do whatever is necessary for the success of the program. I acknowledge that and want you to know that I am tempted to give you a specific figure. But I can't do that. I am convinced that you don't want me to play God for you. Therefore, I must tell you to keep searching for His will. I challenge you to keep searching for ways for God to show His love through you. At some point in the process, you will be comfortable in His will, and at that point, you will do what is right about your financial decision."

We needed a gift of $500,000. Six weeks later, he gave the first million dollar gift his church had ever received. I sincerely believe that twenty years from now he will still remember the joy of that decision because it was made for the right reason.

However, I would be less than candid if I did not point out that it does not always turn out that way. I once sat across the table from a man who had recently sold his business for $168 million. He shared with me that the church building program was important to him, and because it was, he had decided to give $1,500. That's right! Fifteen hundred dollars! Now, if I believe what I say I believe, then I have no real quarrel with that. It is not any of my business. It may be that $1,500 was God's will for him at that time, I don't know. But this I do know: over the years, far more often, it has worked the other way. Far more often, I have seen people who I thought would give $5,000 struggle with their understanding of God's will and then give $50,000.

The important thing to remember is that the highest motivation possible for you or me to give to God's work is not legalism; therefore, those who would seek to motivate us to give can eliminate scary sermons on the wrath of God as a motivational tool. The highest level of motivation is not ego; therefore, they can forget naming buildings after us. The highest motivation is not to reach some high financial target; therefore, they can take the thermometers out of the foyer. The highest motivation is not greed; therefore, they can forget unrealistic promises of sudden riches.

The highest motivation, the motivation that will ultimately lead us to consider seriously the place of material things in our lives, is a spiritual one. This is the desire to know that with the "things" entrusted to us, we have been faithful to the will of God as we understand His will for our lives. It is allowing Him to love and care for His world through the resources that He has placed in our trust.

In 1983, our company, Resource Services, Inc. (RSI) had the opportunity to lead the largest local church fund-raising program in the history of modern Christianity. That program produced $9 million more than the highest stated need. The process of getting to that point illustrates perfectly the motivation of which I speak.

When we were first called to Second Baptist Church in Houston, Texas, to discuss the stewardship program, we were told that the need was for $25 million. With that, it was believed at the time, the total funding needs for the new church could be met. The actual need grew beyond that figure, but that occurred after the stewardship drive was completed. With the $25 million need before us, our staff started the process of designing an approach to challenge the people toward the need.

Bill Wilson, a senior partner in our firm, was given the responsibility of designing the program. Since no church had ever raised that kind of money, he had no pattern to follow. The most any church had ever raised prior to that time had been $17.5 million at First Baptist Church, Orlando, Florida. But, as we reviewed our approach in the Orlando program, it was obvious that the two churches were so different we could not repeat the Orlando approach in Houston.

Frankly, faced with that kind of challenge, we explored every possible approach. We soon realized that even with the experience of the RSI team, we would not be able to develop an approach that would absolutely guarantee results. Someone suggested we just go back to basics. What would be different in this church with its $25 million need from the church with a $200,000 need? People were people, and God's will was God's will, so why shouldn't we stick to the plan in which we had come to believe? Why not just challenge the people to pray and seek the will of God about their giving?

When we finally presented the approach to the Board, I think there was a bit of skepticism. In fact, long after the program was over, the pastor, Dr. Ed Young, said in an interview, "We kept expecting pressure, but these people from RSI kept saying to us that there wasn't going to be any pressure. They just said we were going to have to deal with God about this. So we put it all in His hands, and before long the staff caught what they meant, and then the people caught what they meant, and then the whole church was ablaze.

"Interestingly enough, we had our greatest period of evangelism when we were in the middle of this fund-raising thing."

The technical development of this program was very intense. During the eight-month working period, more than 2,000 people became actively involved in the process. As they became more involved, they also became more receptive to the concept of opening themselves to His leadership in this business of giving. Finally, we came to Victory Sunday. This was two weeks after we had asked the people to begin recording their commitments.

I shall never forget that evening when Mr. John Baugh, founder of the Sysco Corporation and general chairman of the drive, stood before the people to announce that not $25 million, but $30 million had been given. Five million more than the highest stated need!

Now, that is exciting! Indeed, there was tremendous rejoicing, but that is not the end of the story. Listen to what happened over the next few weeks. Within a matter of weeks, weeks *after* the close of the program, just weeks after it had been announced that the people had committed $5 million more than the need, other members of the congregation had stopped by the church office and pledged another $4 million!

Why? The highest goal had already been met. The highest need of the church had already been underwritten.

The answer to that question is best seen in the example of a gift that was made the day after the Victory Service. On the Monday following the announcement of the $30 million being committed, one of the members came to see the pastor. He explained that he had been out of the country for a few weeks and had only returned that morning. He then gave the pastor a commitment card filled out in the amount of $750,000.

Realizing that the gentleman probably had not heard of the announcement the previous night, the pastor explained that the goal of $25 million had been exceeded by $5 million, and that if the man needed to rethink his commitment he should certainly feel free to do so. At that suggestion, the member became indignant. He explained in no uncertain language that his gift was not made because the church needed his money, but rather because he *needed to give!* What he was saying was, "Listen, I got the message. The goal of the program was not to reach $25 or even $30 million. The goal of the program was to walk in God's will."

What a joyous and refreshing reason to give!

In 1993, our firm worked with Southeast Christian Church in Louisville, Kentucky. Again, the goal was extremely aggressive—$26 million. Everyone said that the days of generosity were over. People compared this church to Second Baptist Church in Houston, and came away saying that no church would ever reach those heights in giving again.

Again, Bill Wilson accepted the task of designing the program. Again, considerations related to the poor economy and national uncertainty were examined. Once more, Bill led the design team back to basics.

Once more, he helped the people focus on "God's will through them" rather than reaching a $26 million goal.

And, again, the people responded. In October 1993, the congregation of Southeast Christian Church in Louisville committed over $30 million for the work of the Kingdom. Four million more than the highest stated need and all because God's people were challenged by the right motivation in giving.

It is very important to recognize that, even though there is a high motivation to give, it does not negate the need for an organized structure through which the people can give. Trust me on this one—it doesn't just happen because it is supposed to happen. Again, if I may personalize the point, it has been my experience that I am most receptive to sacrificial giving if I have been actively involved in the giving program. One year we kept records on churches where we made presentations yet the churches' decisions were to "just pray and let God lead the people to give what they wanted to give." In every case, those programs failed to reach their desired objectives. Not one succeeded! What happened? If successful programs result from people seeking and finding God's will for their lives, then why can't they just say "Go and find His will," and by doing that, produce great results?

When you think about it, the reasons that approach doesn't work are evident. First of all, you must analyze what is already happening in the average church. In the average church, only about 20 percent of the membership are participating in a systematic plan of giving. In other words, if your church has 2,000 families, the probabilities are high that if 1,600 of those families never darkened the door of the church again, financially, you would not miss them.

Because of that, the average church has a great majority of people who have no understanding about Christian stewardship at all. They have no concept of giving, and certainly no concept of seeking God's will concerning levels of sacrificial giving. Therefore, the process is not so much a process of giving, but a process of education related to finding and doing the will of God as His will relates to material things in their lives.

I have often told committees that if all they want to do is raise money from the 20 percent of us who already support the church, then just tell us—that group—"Give." That group, the 20 percent, will give whether or not you have an organized program. But if you want to touch the lives of the 80 percent who are not giving, then you must give them a program of education and instruction. For them, the adventure of giving is a new experience. It will not just happen. If they are to be brought into the giving process, they must be actively involved in the organization.

As a part of our ministry, we have had the opportunity to work with many who pastor the largest churches in America. When those pastors are asked to describe self-led programs by churches, there is a general consensus. They agree that the church going through a do-it-yourself program of stewardship will usually raise less than half the amount that could be raised with an outside consultant. If you were to ask them what the RSI team brought to the program in their church that they might not have done on their own, they would say the team brought a pattern of organization that helped move them from the 20 percent into the 80 percent.

Over and over again, that is the experience. Those who may be considered inexperienced stewards must be taught and guided into what, for most of them, is foreign territory. That territory is the "land of the giving."

The organizational process itself is a complex matter. Let me use my home church as a pattern. We have now completed two programs in the church where I am a member. In the last program, we needed to raise $2 million to build a third floor on the educational building and to remodel the current facility.

The first thing we had to do was to calendar the program in such a way as to not be disruptive to the ongoing church programs. Very few churches want to go out of the ministry business to raise money, and certainly our church was no exception. Since we needed five months for the stewardship program, we sat down with every ministry staff member and worked the program calendar around the ministry calendar. When that had been done, we had a calendar that reflected the priority that the church was giving to the stewardship program.

We then started building an organizational structure that would ultimately involve more than 800 people in active participation. Keep in mind that our church had only 1,200 families at the time. Over a period of five months, we conducted over seventy training sessions involving from one to one hundred people at a time.

Certainly, the process was slow. Naturally, it would have been easier to just announce that "Next Sunday is Commitment Sunday—y'all come." That would have been easier, but experience shows it doesn't work. It doesn't work. Because without the organization and the five months of programming and the seventy training sessions, the only people who would have been involved would have been the 20 percent who are always involved. It is a proven fact of stewardship development that not only does it take motivation to have a successful stewardship program, but it also takes a detailed organization that actively involves people.

The final thing that becomes necessary for a stewardship program that successfully challenges and leads people to give sacrificially is to offer opportunities to become creative in giving. Few people have a lot of cash; therefore, if the options in giving can be increased, avenues can be opened that otherwise would not have been considered.

I have seen raw land, developed real estate, jewelry, art objects, yachts, stocks, automobiles, even a registered Hereford bull given in programs under our direction. There is no end to the creativity of God's people when challenged. The profiles of giving in the following chapters are of people who became caught up in the search for God's will, and who, when challenged to find ways to give, did so in creative and imaginative ways. These are people who dared to become seriously involved in a search to determine *what God might want to do through them at this point in their life.* I think you will find their stories interesting.

But the point of all of this is that it doesn't just happen. Stewardship programming and the successful results that follow such a program are as planned and programmed as the great evangelistic crusades that the Billy Graham organization might conduct. They are as biblically-oriented as a course in a great seminary. They are as organized as a great missions conference might be. They are work. They require effort, energy, and resources.

But, oh, the rewards that come from all of the work and the effort. You just have to experience it to know. The happiest people on this earth are the people who, having come to know the will of God for their lives, have learned the great lessons on how to give.

Turn the pages now and read the stories of some who have found that joy. These stories are composites of the thousands who have been moved to give under His leadership. With the exception of the story about Aunt Mamie and Uncle Louie, and the experience with Dr. Jasper Williams, all of the names and places have been changed. Some of these people were a part of programs in large churches where millions of dollars were raised. Others were members of small rural congregations where the numbers were comparatively small. But all of them have a common denominator: in every case, the individual joy and happiness they experienced was worth all of the work and effort.

There is no particular order. The stories can be read at random. My prayer is that as you read about these people, you, too, may begin the process whereby you may come to know the joy of giving.

CHAPTER II

THE FIREPLACE

I remember well the call that came from Dick Hillenger to tell me about the death of Beth Ann's father. Beth Ann was our Banquet Director in a program at High Street Church in San Francisco, and Dick's call was to alert me of the need to get a replacement for her during the time she would be in Alabama attending her father's funeral.

My association with Dick and Beth Ann had been limited to our work together on the church stewardship program, and to dinner on a couple of different evenings in their beautiful home overlooking the magnificent Golden Gate Bridge. On these occasions, the setting was beautiful and the atmosphere warm and cordial. They were truly gracious people who knew how to enjoy the blessings that God had given them.

Dick, a successful architect in the Bay area, was rapidly stamping his imprint in the Bay community. Several large commercial projects bore the imprint of his creativity, even though he had moved to the area to specialize in the residential market. Now, thirteen years later, the name of Dick Hillenger carried weight in the business community.

Beth Ann was making her impact as well.   A
degree from the Bennington School of Design in Atlanta
and a successful run of recognized projects in the Bay
area had established her as a leading home interior
designer. Wisely, they both admitted, they had chosen
not to merge their work even though their careers were
compatible. Each worked on their own projects, and
the parallel success of their careers was an added
blessing they shared.

On the evenings I enjoyed visiting in their home,
I was to learn a great deal about this interesting couple.
On more than one occasion, the conversation centered
around an old wooden fireplace they had chosen to
place in their very modern, contemporary home
overlooking San Francisco Bay. As we sat around the
fireplace on those evenings, they shared the story with
me.

Beth Ann was a country girl in the truest sense of
the word. She was born in the hills of Alabama on a
farm so far back in the hills that Dick often joked that
Beth Ann was raised thirty miles from the nearest sin.
Her parents were hard-working, God-fearing, country
people who worked to see that their only child have
every opportunity possible in life.

As her mother would often say, "I don't want
Beth Ann living in these hills, having six babies, and
dying before she is forty. I want something better for
her."

And it was to that end both she and her husband
worked. Mom and Pop Dooley, as everyone knew

them, with their only child, were a vital part of the community. They enjoyed good neighbors, and in return, they were good neighbors. Once when a family offered to pay Pop Dooley for plowing their garden, he testily replied, "I don't hire out, but if you'll let me neighbor you, then I'll do it for nothin'." Pop Dooley enjoyed "neighboring" people.

The farm was, in the terminology of today, a "working farm." To live there meant getting up with the sun and working late into the night. There were fields to be plowed and cattle to be fed. There were clothes to mend and floors to clean. Beth Ann grew up knowing exactly what work meant. Had she been like so many farm girls of her day, the most vital memories of that part of her life would have been memories to forget.

But it was not so in the Dooley family. For in their house on that farm in Alabama, there was a fireplace that would be the center of good memories for as long as she would live.

The farm had first been homesteaded by her grandfather, Hank Dooley, in the late 1800s. Her father had taken over when her grandfather died in 1927, and he had built the first real house on the property. Additions were made over the years following, and by the time Beth Ann was born, it consisted of either seven or eight rooms—depending on whether or not you counted the "new room out back" which her father had built as a work room.

The living room was a very special place. Here were found the items of life that would best exemplify life in the Dooley household. There were two large overstuffed chairs where her parents would sit after a hard day's work. She and her cousin, Julie, from Writsboro, would sneak around the room when they were little and laugh as they saw Pop sitting in his special chair asleep and snoring loud enough to wake the dead.

Her mother's chair was equally special. Countless were the hours she had spent sitting in her mother's arms listening to this warm and loving woman as she told the stories of angels and saints, of puppies and kittens. Several years before I met Beth Ann, her mother had died. Yet now, years later, as she spoke about her mother, I was always amazed at the smile that appeared on her face. What a special person this country mother must have been.

On the wall in the living room, there was a clock that chimed away the hours. In front of that clock was a Sunday evening ritual that was never missed. After church and just before bedtime on Sundays, Beth Ann and her mother would watch as her father took out the crank and rewound the clock for another week. He would always wind it slowly and then look at them and say, "Well, time is passing. Guess we better make the most of it."

Every Sunday night for as long as Beth Ann could remember that scene took place. Is it any wonder it had a lasting impact on her life?

There were two chairs, a clock, a small table where the Bible sat (one that never needed special dusting because the preacher was coming), and a fireplace.

A fireplace. My, how drab the room would have been without the fireplace.

The mantle had been cut and carved by her grandfather for the new house that his son would someday build and live in with his family. On that mantle sat the memories of a lifetime of love and caring—pictures of Beth Ann on her first horse, the little trophy she had won for the spelling bee. There also sat a genuine, real, fake-cut glass vase that she had won at the county fair and had given to her mother. A more sophisticated mother might have put it away out of sight, but not Beth Ann's. This vase was a gift given in love and would go in a special place for all to see. Later, there would be a place on the mantle for the letters Beth Ann wrote home from college, easily accessible for anyone who wanted to read them over and over again.

After her mother died, her father's health gradually failed to the point that it became impossible for him to live alone. Dick and Beth Ann had insisted he come to San Francisco to live with them, but he chose to move into the local nursing home where so many of his friends now lived.

About every two months, Beth Ann would take a flight from California to Atlanta, rent a car, drive over to see her father, and then return to the life that she had made with Dick in California. It was not the best situation in the world, but everyone involved realized they were all doing the best that they could.

One September day, Dick had business in Atlanta so the two made the trip together. While in the area, they decided to drive out to the old homeplace. As they walked through the house, now abandoned for all useful purposes, the memories suddenly overwhelmed Beth Ann. For a few moments, as Dick held her, she wept uncontrollably.

Later, they sat in two old worn and dusty chairs and talked about the room, but most of all, they talked about the fireplace. The memories soon were fresh and vivid. On that September afternoon, they shared them together and made them real once again. There was the memory of the Christmas morning Beth Ann had gotten her first bike. She was in the second grade, and she just knew that this year Santa would bring her a new bike. She wished and prayed, begged and pleaded her case, and did all the thousand things that an eight-year-old will do to make things happen.

It is hard for an eight-year-old child to understand what hard times are all about. They do not understand what happens when the rains ruin the crops and cattle prices drop to the bottom. All a child knows is that every kid in school will have a new bike.

For a number of months before Christmas, she was aware that her father was never home at night. Whereas before the family enjoyed the time around the fireplace, on these evenings only she and her mother were present. When she would ask about Pop, the answer was always vague.

And then, Christmas morning came. When Beth Ann came into the living room, there was a roaring fire in the fireplace, and standing in front of it was the most wonderful, new red bike that one could imagine. It was all of her dreams rolled into one. For hours she sat on it, pretending that it wasn't 28 degrees outside and that she was riding with her friends. Surely, no one ever had a better Christmas.

Only years later did she learn that on those nights when her father was not at home, he was working a night job in town to earn the money for a new red bike—a present for a daughter whom he loved more than life itself.

That was the kind of joy that the fireplace represented, but not every memory around this special place was a happy one. It was a cold January evening when Beth Ann was fourteen. There had been a knock on the door. A neighbor brought the news of the tragic death of her cousin, Billy, who had been killed when his tractor turned over in a ditch earlier that evening.

Billy and Beth Ann had been close friends. As we sat years later in San Francisco and talked about that event, she could vividly recall all the details of the family gathering around the fireplace as they grieved over his death.

Good and bad, the memories of the fireplace flooded in as Beth Ann shared the details of the life she led before leaving home. But there was one story that seemed to bring extra special joy to her. It was the story of Dick, this city boy from "up north," standing in front of the fireplace in this country farm home. He was the perfect gentleman as he asked Pop Dooley for Beth Ann's hand in marriage.

As Beth Ann told it, she and Dick had met in Atlanta where both were in school. Here he was, an ambitious, young architectural student from New Jersey. And here she was, a farm girl in design school. They had met at a bus stop, of all places, when in typical school-girl style, she had dropped everything she owned in the middle of the street and he had stopped to help her get her act together.

A few days later, he called for a date, and from that first date, it was all over for both of them. After a short two months, he asked her to marry him. In about thirty seconds, she accepted—subject to her father's approval. Country girls from Alabama just do things that way.

On the November evening that Dick was to drive down for dinner, everyone was preparing for his arrival in their own way. Beth Ann had driven home two days before to prepare the way, and by this time she was literally a basket case. If she said one more thing about this guy, Pop Dooley probably would have killed her. Mom Dooley had cooked enough food for a small army and had asked for the tenth time what Dick liked to eat. By the time of his arrival, he could have asked for anything short of a pastrami on rye and she would have had it already prepared for him.

The house had been cleaned until it was immaculate. The mantle, with its accumulation of letters, books, and other plunder, was arranged with every glamorous picture of Beth Ann that had ever been taken.

Pop Dooley was certain that whoever this person was, he was not good enough for his daughter. But Pop Dooley thought he would keep an open mind until after dinner when he would check this guy out.

Finally, Dick arrived, introductions were made, and Mom began the check-out procedures as only a mother can.

What did he expect to do with his life? He wanted to design buildings and be creative in the building world.

Did he go to church? Yes, he was a Methodist, but probably not as active as Beth Ann was. Mom assured him that she would expect that to change!

Where would he and Beth Ann live? In Atlanta, but they had to be open to go anywhere. That did not set well with Pop.

On and on it went all through dinner. A presidential nominee before a congressional committee would not have been asked more questions. Finally, dinner was over, and the men moved to the two big chairs in the living room while the women did the dishes. It was in that thirty minutes that Pop Dooley accepted the fact that this young man would soon be the man to hold first place in his daughter's heart. And like a warrior accepting defeat, he decided that was okay. But, he had to have one last shot as only a future father-in-law could have.

Mom and Beth Ann had come in from the kitchen. Mom took a place at the hearth. Beth Ann sat on the arm of Dick's chair. They visited for a few minutes, and then Pop announced that it was his bedtime. He got up and started out of the room, but as he reached the door, he turned and walked back to the fireplace. Pop put his hand out to Dick and said, "Son, I like you, and I give my blessing to you. But I want you to know something. Do you know what I would do to someone who hurt my daughter?"

"No, sir, I don't," came the reply.

"Well, I'd kill the son of a bitch!" And with that, Pop made his exit.

Such were the experiences of the Dooley family as they shared a fireplace in their small country home in the rural hills of Alabama.

Dick and Beth Ann were married a few months later, and after graduation, they moved to California to begin their life together. Over the years, the changes of life took their toll. Mom died, and Pop moved to the Mountain View Home. The homeplace was rented, with the exception of the house, which gradually fell into disrepair.

Now, after all those years, they sat in the old living room on this September evening and talked about the experiences shared there. It was on this trip that Dick made a suggestion about the fireplace that was readily acceptable to Beth Ann.

They were in the process of building their home overlooking the bay. Plans were being finalized. Dick was completing the architectural design and Beth Ann was bringing the final touches of interior design together. It was a team effort. Therefore, Dick's suggestion was perfectly timed.

"What would you think," he cautiously asked, "of pulling the mantle and hearth of this fireplace out of this house and building them into the den fireplace in our new home?" Beth Ann jumped at the idea! The process was started, and less than six months later when the home in San Francisco was completed, there stood in the den a fireplace filled with wood and memories. Certainly, Dick's idea had been appropriate.

A few days after Dick's call to me concerning the death of Beth Ann's father, she returned and became active in the stewardship drive once again. About four weeks later, I received a call from the pastor saying that Dick and Beth Ann had requested that the two of us come by at the earliest possible time. After checking schedules, we all agreed the pastor and I would go visit with them at their house on the following Thursday evening.

When we arrived, the coffee was already made, a fire was in the fireplace, and it was obvious that Dick and Beth Ann wanted to immediately discuss the reason for the meeting.

"Pastor," Dick began, "over the past few days Beth Ann and I have come to a decision, and we want to discuss it with you. We have asked Ben to be here to help us with the technical details. But rather than me sharing the decision with you, I want Beth Ann to tell you."

We turned to Beth Ann who was now sitting on the hearth accepting the warmth that was flowing from the fireplace. She began slowly, almost as though this was the first time she had thought through the total process.

"Pastor, I am a person who has spent a lifetime enjoying the blessings of God. I had the blessing of being raised in a rural community by godly parents who helped set my values and guided me as I set the course for my life. Then I had the privilege of getting a good education that has enabled me to enjoy a career and lifestyle that is comfortable and rewarding.

"I have a warm, loving husband who shares my life and beliefs. Together, we have a church family that nurtures us and supports us. Life is so very good, and God has blessed us in so many ways.

"Last month, Dick and I went home to bury my father. That act was the final step in sharing his life and the life that he and Mom gave to me.

"Now, as that step has been taken, Dick and I have made a decision. We hope that Mom and Pop would be have pleased. After a lot of thought, we have decided to give the farm in Alabama to our church here in memory of the life that Mom and Dad shared with us. You know, there are about 235 acres there. The house is probably worthless, but the acreage will bring about $200,000. We would like to give the farm to the church, let the church sell it, and use the proceeds in His work."

There was a pause, during which time no one said anything. Then softly, very softly, she continued, "You know, I just think that they will be very pleased with what we are doing."

In the moments that followed, we each sat there thinking our own private thoughts. Each of us sensed that this was a very special moment. I looked at the mantle with all of the scratches and marks of its sixty-plus years. I looked at the hearth where Beth Ann had laughed over a new bike, cried over the death of her cousin, and lovingly looked at the boy from "up north" who was asking for her hand in marriage. I looked at a fireplace and saw the depth of the decision that was being made.

A moment later, Beth Ann spoke again, but this time her voice was strong and her statement was definite. "Yes, sir. They will like this decision. You know, Pastor, I cannot help but believe that all of my life has been prepared for this moment. I wish you could know how good this decision feels."

Then Beth Ann stood and gently placed another log on the fire.

▲ ▲ ▲

AN OBSERVATION

▼ ▼ ▼

In November 1993, our firm completed a capital stewardship program at Southeast Christian Church in Louisville, Kentucky. This church is led by a fine staff of dedicated ministers with Bob Russell serving as senior minister. When we were first approached by their capital funds committee, we were told they wanted to raise $26 million. Once again our faith and experience would be tested.

During the course of their program, we saw God work a mighty work among the people. In fact, about midway through the program, Bob commented in a sermon that there was a great difference between sacrifice and extremism. He wanted to caution the people about making unrealistic commitments while at the same time allowing for God's leadership in their lives. It is often a difficult message to balance.

I remember one Sunday morning when he preached on defining sacrifice. In that sermon, he talked with the people about the miracle that God was doing among them. And then he said, "This is an opportunity to participate in a miracle. This is an opportunity to make a memory for a lifetime and an impact for eternity."

Looking back on it, I think that is what Beth Ann and Dick did that evening before the fireplace. Over the years to come, as they sit before the fire, they will never be far from the memory of the decision made there on that extraordinary evening. And the end result of that decision will impact the lives of others for eternity.

CHAPTER III

GHOSTS AND GAMBLING

I must admit I had certain reservations concerning the inclusion of this story. First of all, I do not fully understand ghosts, and secondly, I do not believe in gambling. This story is about both. I would be less than candid if I did not explain from the beginning that I do not understand all that happened; therefore, I will be better off simply reporting the facts as I saw them, unveil rather than trying to make a big, exciting story out of it.

Also, I will admit from the beginning that I do not fully understand how a state lottery works, so the details of this experience may be a bit loose, but the general facts are accurate.

Remember now, we are considering ghosts and gambling.

In the fall of 1985, we were retained by the Sunset Community Church in Haversville, New York, to lead a major fund-raising drive for a new sanctuary. The church had a budget income of $484,000 and needed to raise around $3 million to build the building that was then on the drawing board.

Because of the size of the church membership, and because a rather large amount of money was needed to build the building, we made a detailed analysis of the membership. As we examined the membership, we determined from our years of experience that if we were to raise the amount needed, a gift of $500,000 would be an absolute necessity.

Two facts made this true. First of all, the church had a very small membership base. There were only 650 potential giving families. This simply meant there would be a need for very large gifts to make up for the fact that there was not a large base from which to draw. Secondly, the church membership was very young and young couples tend to be pretty well-stretched in their obligations. Often when a church has a profile of young adults, the ability to give may be a reflection of their age rather than their dedication. In that case, large gifts are necessary.

All of those factors were present at Sunset Community Church. So in building the case statement for the fund drive, we indicated at the start of the program that a gift in the $500,000 range was an absolute necessity if $3 million was to be raised. We then proceeded to present our findings to the Board and begin our work. We did so with an air of pessimism because every person on the Board felt that the possibility of such a gift was very remote. Nevertheless, work was begun on the program.

Often we tell a church that we can never create "potential." If the "potential" for a $500,000 gift is not there, then there is nothing any of us can do about it.

We can sometimes create the "desire" to give, but "potential"—never. We realized that in a special way at Sunset Community Church. They were good people. They were willing to work hard and give the program everything necessary to succeed, but they were not wealthy people. All these factors would be taken into account as we set goals for the program.

The goal-setting process is not taken lightly at RSI. We recognize that the perception of success for the church will ultimately be related to their commitments in relationship to goals that have been set. For example, if a church has the potential to raise only $1 million, and we set the goal at $2 million, we are setting them up to fail. Even if through great sacrifice they raise over $1 million, but still fail to reach the $2 million goal, their perception is one of failure. If, however, that same church had set a goal of $1 million and then raised $1.2 million, their perception of the results would be of great victory.

Maybe it should not be like that, but in reality it is. So when the committee at RSI came together to discuss goals for Sunset Community Church, we took into consideration the fact that the church needed a victory. Therefore, we recommended a top goal of $2 million.

In the course of discussion with the Board, I indicated that while this would be short of the $3 million needed to build the sanctuary, it would put them in position to build the building. However, a short-term loan for the final $1 million might be needed.

Brad Williams, a young businessman in the church and Chairman of the Board, finally asked me what I thought the odds were of raising $3 million.

"Without the $500,000 lead gift that could be used to influence probably another $200,000 to $300,000, I think it is almost impossible," I said.

"But what would it take," he persisted, "to hit the $3 million without a $500,000 gift?"

"A miracle," I replied. "Brad, I really think that it would take a miracle."

With that, the Board voted to set a fourth goal, a top goal, and they called it "The Miracle Goal." No one was more convinced that it would take a miracle than this consultant.

Very often when goals are announced, the tendency is to forget the lower goals and focus only on the top goal—in this case "The Miracle Goal." To his credit, when he presented the goals to the congregation, Brad was very frank and forthright about the top goal.

Speaking to the congregation, he said, "Unless something dramatic happens, we may not reach the $3 million goal, but we want you to know that is the need. The consultants working with us tell us that to reach that goal we must have a gift of $500,000. Frankly, at this point, we do not know whether that is a possibility, but if it is, then we should go for it. We have named that goal our "Miracle Goal" because we know that to reach it will indeed take a miracle."

Most churches have one person who is a bit eccentric, and at Sunset Community Church, it was Miss Tilly Simpson. Miss Tilly was not a wealthy person by any means. She lived alone in her small, white-frame house, went to church every Sunday, bought one New York state lottery ticket each week, and talked to her dead husband, George, who had gone to be with the Lord in 1967. Other than that, she was a perfectly normal member of the Sunset Community fellowship.

After the goals were announced that Sunday morning, she met Brad at the door. "Brad," she began, "let's go for that Miracle Goal. I do not know where that $500,000 gift will come from, but tonight I'll ask George. He's an accountant, you know, so I'm sure he can work it out."

With that, she turned to leave, leaving one very astonished Board chairman in her wake. That night, at the monthly Board meeting, Brad reported that the problem of reaching the goal was over. Miss Tilly was going to talk to George about it and after all, "He's an accountant, you know."

Over the next few weeks as the program progressed, the words of Miss Tilly were soon forgotten. The activities continued on schedule, and from the viewpoint of the consultant team assigned to the project by RSI, everything was right on target for a $2 million success. That would be over the top goal as projected by us. Not the "Miracle Goal" you understand, but no one, not even the church leadership, really expected that one to be reached—that is, unless a miracle occurred.

Two weeks before the program was over, Brad got a call from Miss Tilly asking him to drop by her house after work. Since she was in his deacon ministry group and was due for a call anyway, Brad figured this was a good way to kill two birds with one stone. He would go by after work, make his deacon visit, and find out why she wanted to see him at this particular time. He always enjoyed the visits with Miss Tilly, even though she was, in his terms, "as nutty as a fruitcake." Besides that, it was always interesting to get her latest message from George. You remember George, died in 1967—he was an accountant, you know.

After the obligatory cookies and coffee, Miss Tilly began to move to the serious subject of gambling. "Brad," she confessed, "I have a terrible sin to confess. I am a gambler."

Brad held back a smile as he pictured Miss Tilly sitting at a poker table with a green visor, looking through smoke and betting on an inside-straight.

"It's true, Brad. Every week I go right down to Murphy's store and I buy a lottery ticket. I know it's wrong, but I just do it. I just put down my dollar and pick my numbers and hope for the best. I've never won. I don't know why I do it, but I do.

"George used to bet the horses, you know, and we had awful fights about it, but he hasn't done that in years."

Since he had been dead for eighteen years, Brad almost lost it on that one. How do you reform a horse-bettor, he thought? You have him die in 1967!

"Well now, Brad, here is why I had to talk to you today," Miss Tilly continued. "Last night, when I was talking to George, I was telling him about the need at the church and about how we really needed a gift of $500,000. You know, George understands numbers like that, and after he thought about it for a little bit, he came up with the answer.

"He said that the only way we were ever going to get that kind of money was for someone to win it in the lottery. Well, right then and there I knew that was the answer, so I asked him exactly what numbers I should play.

"After a little while, he came back and said for me to play Brad Williams' birth date, plus the numbers 22, 28, and 13. So, Brad, George and I need to know your birthday."

By this time, Brad was about ready to call the men with the white coats, but then he saw how very serious Miss Tilly was about all of this. Reluctantly, he gave her his birth date: 11-19-47.

"Great!" exclaimed Miss Tilly. "Our number next week will be 22-28-13-11-19-47. Brad, I just know that this is it. Whatever is won on this ticket, I will give it to the building fund."

As he was leaving to get in his car, Brad felt that he should have taken the time to teach a lesson in morality. But when the student reaches seventy-three years of age, bets one dollar a week on the lottery, and carries on a conversation at night with a man who has been dead for eighteen years, it doesn't seem likely that the lesson would take.

The story of Miss Tilly and her message from George became the tension-relief valve that the Steering Committee needed as the final days of the program approached. As the meetings would begin, someone would usually say, "Well, we don't have to worry about the big one. George has taken care of that one for us!" And the meeting would settle down to the business at hand.

Frankly, business at hand was not going so poorly. In spite of the demographics of the congregation, a few good things were happening. We were beginning to realize the church might very well raise over the $2 million mark—an outstanding feat for a church predominantly made up of young couples and with an ongoing income of less than $500,000.

In the meantime, Miss Tilly had taken George's advice to heart. On the Tuesday before the Sunday night banquet, she had gone to Murphy's corner store and bought a ticket with the numbers 22-28-13-11-19-47 plainly marked. The weekly jackpot was over $2 million, and if this ticket won, Miss Tilly would be faithful to her promise. Every dime would go to the church as a gift from her and George. In her mind, it was as good as done.

On the Saturday night before the banquet, she sat glued to the television set waiting for the announcement of the weekly numbers. When the numbers were announced, she almost had a heart attack. George was right! They had won!

Quickly, she ran to the phone to call Brad. Looking his name up in the church directory, she carefully dialed and got "one of those old message machines." Normally she would not talk to one of those old things. If people could not answer their own phone, they should just let it ring. But tonight was special, and so waiting for Brad's recorded greeting to end, she decided to make an exception and leave a message on the machine.

"Brad Williams, this is Miss Tilly," she said trying to hide her excitement. "George won! I do not believe it, but George was right. George won! Everything won on that ticket will go to the church. We can build the sanctuary. Tomorrow morning I will be at church and I will bring the ticket. It all goes to the church. George was right. I just knew George would be right. He's such a smart man, you know."

With that, she hung up the phone—or at least she thought she did. She failed to seat the receiver properly, and for the next two hours as Brad frantically tried to get back in touch with her, he was met by the constant buzz of the busy signal.

Turning on the 11:00 p.m. news, Brad saw the weekly winning numbers flash across the screen. Sure enough, there was the string of six numbers and they did indeed include that magic birth date series: 11-19-47. There was also the announcement that a ticket with the winning numbers for the $2 million jackpot had been won.

A quick call to the pastor and they realized that no one knew the other three numbers Miss Tilly had played. It was evident that no one had taken her seriously, and it was equally evident that the resolve of the church leadership against gambling was weakening.

By the time the next morning arrived, the entire Steering Committee had been alerted. They had never been to church so early in their lives, but no one wanted to miss what was about to happen.

As soon as Miss Tilly walked in the door, she was ushered into the pastor's office where she was to face the entire Steering Committee. Smiling like the cat that ate the mouse, Miss Tilly played it to the hilt. She recounted in painful detail her entire conversation with Brad that day in her sitting room and she explained how George had told her to call Brad and get his birth date to use on the ticket.

On and on she went, and with every word the committee thought they would die. They wanted to yell, "Miss Tilly! Just let us see the ticket!"

And finally she did. With the newspapers spread on the pastor's desk and the pages turned to yesterday's winning numbers, Miss Tilly laid her ticket down. One by one they matched the numbers, and one by one they saw that Miss Tilly, with George's wise counsel, had indeed been a winner. She had won the grand total of $50!

With the flare that comes from staying awake all night to figure out just how to do it right, Miss Tilly took an envelope from her purse, placed the ticket in it, and gave it to the pastor. On the envelope was written, "To Sunset Community Church: the total value of this winning ticket to help build the new sanctuary. From: George and Tilly Simpson."

After the shock of it all, and after no small amount of disappointment, a few of the people on the Steering Committee thought through what had happened. Now George knew the program needed a gift of $500,000. He spoke to Miss Tilly and helped her find a winning ticket. That ticket won $50. George was only one comma and four zeros off. As someone later said to the committee, "I knew George. He really wasn't very good with numbers."

The church went on to raise $2.3 million for the new sanctuary. The commitments came in all sizes from a broad base of people. There were no particular miracles except the miracle of the people sacrificing together to build the House of God. And yes, the $2.3 million included George and Miss Tilly's winning ticket.

▲ ▲ ▲

AN OBSERVATION

▼ ▼ ▼

The program at Sunset Community Church is a mirror image of thousands of others I have witnessed over the years. At RSI, our reputation is enhanced by the great multimillion dollar programs that receive national publicity.

Time magazine did a piece on the $34 million program at Second Baptist Church in Houston. The Florida papers went overboard to tell the story of the $17.5 million success at First Baptist Church, Orlando. At RSI, we have had the privilege to conduct programs in over twenty churches that raised in excess of $10 million. So it is in that area that we have become known as America's leading church fund-raising organization.

But in reality, that is not where most of our ministry takes place. Most of the churches where we work are average, small evangelical churches with budgets of a few hundred thousand. In those programs, we very seldom get a $1 million gift. The programs don't get a lot of publicity. But the success is just as real.

Most programs succeed simply because hundreds of people work hard, care, and sacrifice to make them succeed. I am very glad God doesn't support His church through the lottery. I am also grateful that He uses people just like you and me to see His purpose carried out in this world.

CHAPTER IV

A LIFETIME OF WEALTH

I f someone should be so bold as to ask you to give away everything you have earned in your lifetime, no doubt you would think them a bit strange. After all, most of us in America have measured our lives by the "things" we have accumulated over the years.

This story is about a 59-year-old man who made the decision to give it all away.

I first met James V. Robertson III in his office in downtown Denver on January 12, 1988. He was a senior partner in one of the most prestigious law firms in the country. At the request of his pastor, we had gone to seek his advice about the building program which was to be launched in the church.

It was no secret that Mr. Robertson was not overly excited about the steps being taken by his church at this time. By Board action, the church was going to build a new educational wing, although Mr. Robertson, a Board member, was not in favor of that move.

In his opinion, the church needed a new sanctuary far more than additional educational space. He had made a strong case for the sanctuary, but had been unable to sway the Board in his direction. As a result, when the crucial vote came, he found himself on the losing side. Mr. Robertson was not accustomed to losing.

So how does one move from opposition to the program to a point of sacrificial commitment? The progression of that decision is an interesting one. To fully understand it in the life of this individual, it is necessary to consider the influence of four women in his life. Allow me to introduce them one by one.

Everyone knew that little Jimmy Robertson's mother was a bit strange. One of her friends once described her as being "the only person I ever knew who could ultimately see depression in every one of life's positive events."

Another said of her, "Mrs. Robertson was a kind lady, but she was the most negative person I have ever known. Somehow she just always knew that disaster was going to be around the very next corner."

A friend of mine has described this kind of person as being afflicted with the Depression Era Syndrome. These are people who grow up with the needs and struggles of the Great Depression, and are now convinced that no matter how good things are going, they will always get worse. It is rather the Ziggy mentality.

Little Jimmy was taught that you work hard, you save, and you don't enjoy your earnings because the fact is that one day, totally unrelated to your control, you will lose it all. This great life lesson was reinforced often by his mother's incomplete statement, "I'm glad that it is going well for you now, because you just never know.... "

Indeed, little Jimmy's mother had a great influence on his life and the formulation of his life's philosophy and values.

Living two houses down from Jimmy was the second person who influenced the values of this young man. Her name was Cindy, and she was the most beautiful girl Jimmy Robertson had ever known. Maybe when you are in the fourth grade it doesn't make a lot of difference if you have braces on your teeth and freckles on your nose. If you are the first love of a bashful boy down the street, he will see nothing but stars. Such was the view of Cindy through the eyes of Jimmy Robertson.

Now, when you are in the fourth grade and trying to get the attention of your first love, you do strange and interesting things. You try to make certain you are in front of the school yard when she starts home so that you can just happen to be going the same way. You act weird. You cross your eyes and tell funny stories. You call her four times in one evening to get the next day's English assignment. Love in the fourth grade is a special brand of love. And because it is, you cannot wait for Valentine's Day.

In Jimmy's fourth grade homeroom, there was to be a special box, and everyone was to bring their Valentines to place in the box. You bought the kind that came in a package of twenty-five for a dollar, and you gave one to everyone in the class.

But if there was someone special, someone with braces on her teeth and freckles on her nose, you went all out and bought the biggest box of candy you could find—the kind in the huge, heart-shaped box with the flower on top. And you gave it to her at recess when everyone in the class could see that she was your girl. Yes, love in the fourth grade is a special kind of love.

Jimmy spent all afternoon at Engle's Drugstore looking at the box of candy. It was the big one with the white flower and it even came with a special card. It cost $3.95. Jimmy knew that in all of his life he had never had that much money at one time. But somehow, maybe if he explained how much it meant, his mother would be a little more generous and let him have the money. After all, this was not a luxury. When you are in the fourth grade and you're in love and it's the day before the Valentine party, this is an absolute necessity.

He knew the answer almost before he got the request out of his mouth. The answer came in the form of a twenty-minute lecture on the value of money. You do not spend money on "mess" like that. You never know when you will need something important, and then what would you have?

He knew the lecture. He just thought that when you are in love and in the fourth grade and your total world depends on everyone knowing that Cindy is your girl—well, he thought it might be different. It wasn't.

That night, he counted his life's savings. Total: $1.07. For that, he couldn't buy the biggest box, but he could buy a heart-shaped box. No flower or card you understand, but if Cindy felt like he did, then it would be okay.

The next morning when Mr. Engle opened his store, Jimmy was at the door waiting. This was the day. The party was at 2:30 p.m., and by 2:45 p.m. everyone would know that Cindy was his girl. All of the Valentines would be placed in the big box. But if you had a special gift, it would be placed by the side, and if you wrote your name big enough, everyone would know who was giving which box. Valentine's Day in the fourth grade is really "the big time."

Was there ever a moment when you were a kid that you wanted to die? For little Jimmy Robertson, it came at 2:42 p.m. on February 14 in his fourth grade homeroom with all of his classmates looking at the cards on all of the Valentine boxes. For it was at that moment that he read the name on the card that had been placed on the biggest and most beautiful box of candy that he had ever seen in his life. The card simply read, "To Cindy, From Jerry—I love you."

That beautiful box with the big white flower was sitting right beside the little, plain, red heart box with a card big enough for all of his friends to see. That card said, "To Cindy, From Jimmy—I love you."

Someone later said that Cindy had come over to Jimmy and said, "Jimmy, did you see what Jerry gave me? It's bigger than any box here. Oh, I like your box, too. Thank you very much."

But that day, Cindy walked home with Jerry. And on that day, little Cindy, with the braces on her teeth and freckles on her nose, had no idea how much she had influenced the life of James V. Robertson III.

By the time Jim had reached high school, fourth grade memories had been buried to play their silent influences over the years to come. The high school years were filled with the usual turmoil of being a teenager. Jim Robertson, with his good looks and keen mind, had a bit of an edge on everyone else.

But for those who knew him well, there was a drive, an aggressive determination that seemed to set him apart. Some of the guys in high school wanted to succeed, but it was as though Jim had to. One cannot help but wonder where it all would have taken him had it not been for Miss Molly.

Miss Molly Becker had always taught high school English. No one remembered when she started teaching, and most never expected to see her cease teaching. Miss Molly was as close to being an institution as Jim's little hometown had ever seen.

It happened one day after class when Jim stopped to ask Miss Molly a question about the final paper he was writing. It was one of those casual moments that most good teachers give to their students that may, as it did in this case, influence that student for life.

Years later, Jim would find it difficult to reconstruct the statement made to him that day, but it went something like this: "Jim, I've had my eye on you and I want you to know something. If you get a good education and channel that wonderful drive you have built within, I believe you can have anything you want in this world. If you want money or fame or prestige, I really believe it can be yours. I want you to know that I am pulling for you."

Now that was not the statement that Jim would remember verbatim years later. The statement that he would remember word for word came after he had responded to her encouragement in the only way he knew how. He phrased it like his mother might have phrased it when he replied, "I know that I could, Miss Molly, but what difference does it make? In this world, even if you make it, you just lose it again. It's totally out of your control."

Miss Molly looked at him for a moment and then spoke the words that would begin a complete change in the direction of Jim Robertson's life. She said, "Jim, I know all your life you have been taught that. I don't have a better friend in the world than your mother, and I know how she has taught you that. But, Jim, listen to me. That's a lie! Life, and whatever you want to make of it, is in your control. It is totally in your control. I will be interested to see what you do with it."

College and law school followed high school. In the final year of law school, he married Shirley Moore who pledged to love him "in sickness and in health, in poverty as in wealth." There followed a growing law practice, two children, house payments, and all those things that people work so hard to accumulate.

To say that Shirley was a major influence in his life during those early years of his career would be to give more credit to her than one probably should. She was there, but he was such a dynamic force that she was almost an appendage to his life and not necessarily a vital part of it. It was not until crises arrived that she became the fourth major female influence in his life.

In the eighth year of their marriage, Jim faced a major business crisis. A business partner signed away the assets of their law firm without Jim's knowledge, and then the "deal that could not go bad" did.

At 33 years of age with a wife and two children, he was to face the frightening reality: maybe Mama was right.

It was during one of those late night pillow conversations that Shirley was to mark her place in his life. As they thought through all that was happening to them, it was Shirley, who in a quiet wisdom that comes from one who sees the facts below the surface of immediate realities, brought him back to where he needed to be.

"Jim, don't forget what Miss Molly told you," she reminded him. "If you want it to be, it really is in your control."

That simple statement from a rather simple and noncomplex person started a profound thought process in the mind of Jim Robertson.

"If I am in control, then I can choose to ask for help in solving these problems. If I control the request for help, then it is not out of weakness but out of wisdom that I can make that choice. Therefore, not as a plea from weakness, but rather as an acknowledgement of my ability to determine my own destiny, I now choose to ask God to become my partner."

For Jim Robertson, that was the end of the discussion. Life in the second half was now to begin.

◆

On January 12, 1988, James V. Robertson III was on the Board of the church. He sat in his downtown law office and shared with the pastor and me his feelings about the project and the steps that the Board had taken. He was against the building project.

He summed it all up by saying something like this:

"Pastor, years ago when I made the decision to partner with God, I learned that He doesn't always ask for my opinion. He does ask me to be faithful. My commitment to you is that, over the next few months, Shirley and I will seriously consider a search for God's will in this matter of our support for the building program. You have my word on that."

Three months later, he stood before the entire congregation to share his experience.

"Over the years, I have spent most of my life looking at money and material things from two different perspectives. First of all, how could I make more? There is within me a built-in drive reinforced with many life experiences that I don't want to be poor. I have worked hard all of my life to see that did not happen.

"Second, I was taught almost from birth that you must not get accustomed to money because at any moment you might lose it. So I have spent a great deal of my life protecting wealth for fear that God or the bank might repossess it all.

"Last month, Shirley and I decided to play it a different way. We asked ourselves the question, 'What would happen if, rather than living in fear that it might be taken, we just gave it all away? What could . . . what would the result be?'

"Well, we don't know, but we are going to find out. Last week we had our accountant figure up our net worth. The total came to $1,680,924. This is the accumulation of a thirty-five-year career and a thirty-three-year marriage.

"Our commitment to the building program is that over the next three years, we will give a sum equal to our current net worth. I want you to know that we feel so very good about that decision.

"I had a dear, sweet high school teacher who once said to me, 'Jim Robertson, life and whatever you want to make of it is totally in your control.'

"I stand here before you this morning to attest to the fact that Miss Molly was 100 percent correct."

▲ ▲ ▲
AN OBSERVATION
▼ ▼ ▼

I do not know how to explain, nor do I care to attempt to explain, the decision of a person willing to do so much for the Kingdom of God. While the story of Jim Robertson is a story of unusual sacrifice, it is also a story that has been repeated more than once.

Several years ago we conducted a capital stewardship program for The First Presbyterian Church in Houston, Texas. Here was a church with less than a $2 million annual budget that wanted to raise over $7.5 million. That would be a miracle by any measure.

As the program developed, I was sitting in the office of a very prominent leader in the church. This individual was at a very comfortable position in life. God had been good to him over the years.

But on this day, there was a sense of absolute peace about him as he shared with me his decision about the stewardship program. He shared some of the struggle of his early life and how over the years God had blessed his business.

He told me about the discussion he had with his wife the evening before and how they had prayed to know God's will in this decision about giving. And then he said, "Ben, after our family discussion last night, we made a decision. As a result of that decision, I called my accountant this morning and asked him to begin calculating my net worth as of commitment Sunday next week.

"After a lot of prayer we have decided to give a figure equal to our net worth." After pausing for a few minutes, he quietly concluded, "We just want to see what God will do with a 57-year-old businessman who is willing to start over with Him."

I have often thought about that conversation and compared it to the selfish decade the country has recently experienced. It is then that I most want to shout to the masses, "They were not all like that. They were not all selfish and self-centered. There were some whose sacrifice was so profound, whose commitment was so strong, and whose love for Christ was so intense that they gave with no thought of personal gain. And some were willing to give it all!"

CHAPTER V

PLEASE, GOD, GIVE ME
ANOTHER CHANCE

S omeone has described flying as hundreds of hours of boredom interspersed with a few moments of absolute terror. On February 11, 1983, Bill Martin would attest to the validity of that statement. Bill's moment of terror came at exactly 2:56 p.m. It was a moment he would not soon forget.

Later, when I talked with him about the experience and he related the events of that moment, I found his answer to one question particularly interesting. The question: "What one thought pops into your mind when you think of that experience?" The answer: "My first thought is of a prayer of desperation and total helplessness that I expressed in that moment, 'Dear God, please give me another chance.'"

Bill told me the story as we sat on the patio of his summer home in Colorado. We looked out over snow-capped Buffalo Mountain as he recalled the way it started.

All his adult life, Bill Martin had wanted to learn to fly an airplane. For some people, flying is a necessity. For Bill, it was to become a passion. When he was in college, he had his first encounter with a salty, old flying instructor in Denver. Walking out to a twenty-year-old Piper J-3 on a hot Saturday afternoon, he had heard the instructor explain the importance of the cockpit instruments.

"Don't ever trust your instincts. Don't ever assume that you know more than the plane. You must rely on your altimeter to tell you how high you are. You must trust your turn-and-bank indicator to let you know the position of the plane in relation to the earth. A compass will point you in the right direction. Don't ever try to outthink them. If you are going to fly, you must learn to totally trust your instruments."

The point well made, they approached the plane that would be used for training. Only the instructor had more miles than the plane. With total horror, Bill looked into the cockpit at a panel that was totally devoid of instruments.

"You remember what I said about instruments? Well, don't forget. If this plane had an altimeter, it would be in that hole right there. If we had a turn-and-bank indicator, it would be right there. Right there is where the compass would go." With that, he motioned Bill into the plane.

With all of the skills of a crop duster, the instructor took off. He landed 30 minutes later with one very sick, frightened, and disillusioned prospective student.

It was exactly seven years later that Bill obtained the name of a reputable flying school with a professional instructor and started the process all over again. One month later, he made that first solo flight, and once again, he was hooked on the freedom of flight.

Over the years as his business grew, he found the airplane to be a tremendous business tool as well as a luxury. He found it was now possible for him to have a meeting five hundred miles away and still be home by bedtime. He could fly out in the morning, meet with a client, and still return home for the five o'clock news.

Bill and his wife, Sue, lived in Denton, Texas, at that time. Though she did not share his enthusiasm for flying, she did understand the freedom it gave Bill. Her only concern was the fact that Bill was not instrument rated. His legal flying was limited to clear days and starlit nights. His nonlegal flying caused him to occasionally get caught in a thunderstorm or to take off at night when the fog was only a "little thick."

Sue pushed hard for the instrument training that would provide Bill with a degree of expertise that would not only make him legal to fly in all kinds of weather, but would also teach him to "fly blind" if he had to, using only the instruments in the plane. This plane had a full set of instruments.

Finally, after a few months of discussion, Bill took four weeks off and went to instrument flight school. That training was the most difficult study he had ever known. Eight hours a day of classroom work, followed by endless hours of homework, coupled with hours of rigorous flying tests soon made an impression on Bill. These people were serious about this. When he completed the course and passed his check ride, he, too, understood that a license to fly in all kinds of weather did not automatically become a license to be careless and stupid.

Bill came home a licensed instrument pilot with a new respect for his plane and especially the environment in which it operated. For the next ten years, that respect paid dividends. Yet, twice during that ten years, Bill became careless about the details of flying. And on both occasions, that carelessness almost cost him his life.

The first event took place one evening about 10:00 p.m. after a long day of business meetings in Little Rock, Arkansas. Bill had flown out in his own plane, a Cessna 182 that he had bought three years before from a local doctor in Dallas. He had over 1,400 hours flying in that plane, and he cared for it like it was a member of his family.

When he arrived back at the airport in Little Rock to file his flight plan to Denton County Airport, he found a beautiful night sky. A full moon filled the sky to the extent that he knew this flight would be almost like flying on a clear day. Because of this, he made his first mistake.

A briefer at Flight Service in Little Rock explained that the Ft. Worth radar was down and it would be two hours before he could get a flight plan approved. Looking at the bright moon, thinking about getting home and not wanting to wait two hours to leave, Bill decided to forego a flight plan and simply take off. Perfectly legal—not particularly smart.

Any good pilot always checks his plane after the ground service crew has serviced it. The plane had been refueled by the ground crew that afternoon, and Bill decided to get his flashlight out and do a "walk-around." He got the flashlight out, hit the switch—and nothing happened. Dead batteries! A quick glance at the office showed him the ground crew was fueling another plane and would not be able to help him for a few minutes.

So, with the complete rationalization that the plane was always serviced well and that he had never had any trouble with it, he threw the useless flashlight into the back seat. As he climbed into the plane, he had an uneasy feeling. But like so many pilots before him, he overrode the feeling. He started the engine and called for clearance to taxi. Bill Martin had just made mistake number two.

At thirty-five minutes into the flight, Bill was at six thousand feet, thinking of home, and beginning to smell the faint burn of hot motor oil. Since the senses tend to play tricks on pilots in single-engine planes flying alone at night, Bill thought little about the smell of oil. Certainly, he did not consider the fact that a careless ground crew member might have left the oil filler cap off, thus allowing the oil to drain from the engine. The plane was not so easily fooled.

Thirty-seven minutes into the flight, a casual glance at instruments that had been too long ignored indicated Bill had real problems. Thirty-eight minutes into the flight and the engine—the only engine—froze. At 6,000 feet on a clear moonlit night somewhere over southwest Arkansas, a motorized Cessna 182 became a powerless glider. That wasn't the way Bill had planned to end the day.

He realized that because he had not filed a flight plan, no one would look for him. He realized that by not checking his oil, he had made a potentially fatal mistake. He realized that in about seven minutes he would find out how well the Cessna could land in treetops.

Bill Martin was a lucky man. Setting up a glide path that would give him his best glide rate, he started to look for a place to set the plane down. Seven minutes later, he landed in a plowed field. He walked to a farm house, called his wife, accepted a bed, and went to sleep.

The next morning he walked back to his plane. In the night landing he had missed power lines by less than 10 feet. He had landed in the only open field in about a 20-mile area and his plane was unharmed. The only scratch on Bill was caused by the barbed-wire fence he'd climbed through to get to the house where he had seen lights.

Bill never once considered thanking God for his luck. Sitting on the patio in Colorado, I asked him if he had been scared.

"No," he answered. "I never really thought that I couldn't handle it. Not that one, at least. But let me tell you about another time. February 11, 1983, to be exact. That was the day that I realized that Bill Martin couldn't do it all. It was the most frightening day of my life!"

It seems that Sue took the night landing experience more seriously than did Bill. She began to review her life and to reconsider some of the things she had gotten away from as an adult. She began attending a small community church in Denton. She started valuing the time she and Bill had together. For the first time, she started to say a prayer for Bill when he was flying. Life was changing for her. And while Bill respected that change, he just didn't change with her. He recognized that the changes started as a result of his night landing. What Sue didn't understand, and that Bill did understand, was that Bill always had it under control. Why change your life if you always have things under control?

On February 11, 1983, at 2:56 p.m., Bill learned what it meant to be out of control. There is probably no sensation on earth like the sensation of flying an airplane in total instrument conditions. In those conditions when there is no visual reference to the ground, the mind is easily fooled. You could be upside down and never know it. On a routine flight out of Memphis, Bill was to find out firsthand how powerful the mind could be.

Bill had left Denton, Texas, for Memphis, Tennessee, around 7:00 a.m. He had flown to

Memphis for an early lunch and was scheduled to fly to Houston, Texas that afternoon. The morning flight was uneventful. He had filed an instrument flight plan out of Denton, climbed to 7,000 feet, and flown on top of the cloud deck in perfectly clear, sunny skies.

By this time, Bill had purchased another single-engine plane, a Piper Lance. The Lance is a six-passenger plane that is known for being a real workhorse. Bill had about 1,200 hours flying in this particular plane, a plane he had bought new almost two years earlier.

When he arrived in Memphis, he immediately filed an instrument flight plan for a 12:45 p.m. departure for Houston. He was told in the customary weather briefing that southwest Arkansas and southeast Texas were both in the grips of a stationary warm front that was causing fog and drizzle over the entire area. Houston was overcast with five-mile visibility, but en route he would pass over areas where the cloud ceiling was near ground level and the fog was causing visibility to drop to zero. It was not a good day for flying, but not totally unacceptable for an instrument pilot with over 2,000 hours.

A recheck of the weather after lunch indicated things had not changed a great deal. Houston was holding up, Memphis was well above minimums for takeoff, and Bill's meeting in Houston that had been scheduled for four months was still on.

At 12:53 p.m., Bill was cleared for takeoff from Memphis. Memphis tower passed him off to Memphis

Center, and he was cleared to climb to 10,000 feet. The tops of the clouds had been reported at 8,500 so he expected to top out at about nine minutes into the flight. He was not carrying any passengers or luggage, so the Lance was performing with a lot of horses and not much of a load. The climb was uneventful.

One can never be sure of a weather report that is more than one minute old, so Bill was not surprised when he never did reach those cloud tops which had been reported at 8,500. Ten thousand feet was as socked in as 5,000, so he just resigned himself to flying for the next few hours on total instruments—not unusual or even dangerous in itself, but certainly not what he preferred.

At 1:43 p.m., Memphis Center passed him off to Houston Center. Bill, in N2830L (30L), began transmissions with Houston Center (HOU). The following is an exact record of those conversations.

30L: "Houston, this is 2830 Lima with you at 10,000 feet."

HOU: "Roger, 2830 Lima, squawk 2367. El Dorado altimeter is 29.36."

30L: "Squawking 2367. Level 10,000. Understand 29.36."

HOU: "2830 Lima, radar contact."

With this contact made, the flight would settle into a normal pattern of talking only when necessary, the pilot busy watching the gauges and flying the airplane. That is the way it is supposed to happen. The conversation recorded beginning at 2:28 p.m. indicated someone was not following the plan.

30L: "Houston, 2830 Lima. I have a slight problem here. Level 10,000 feet with a very rough engine. I'm a single-engine Lance with one soul aboard."

HOU: "Roger, 2830 Lima. Understand you're having engine trouble. Please keep us advised."

2:34 p.m.

30L: "Houston, 2830 Lima. I've got some real problems here. I'm showing 23 DME (miles) from Lufkin. Say Lufkin weather, please."

HOU: "2830 Lima. Lufkin weather last hour—ceiling obscure, visibility 1/16 in light rain and fog. Lufkin altimeter is 29.94."

30L: "Roger, Houston. Understand 29.94."

2:38 p.m.

30L: "Houston, 2830 Lima. Can't hold altitude. (Garbled transmission)."

HOU: "2830 Lima. Understand losing altitude.
        State intentions. Several instrument aircraft
        in your area."

HOU: "2830 Lima. Lufkin Flight Service has
        advised current weather: ceiling obscure,
        visibility zero. Wind calm. Current
        altimeter 29.94."

2:40 p.m.

30L: "Houston, 2830 Lima. Clear it out under
        me. I'm going down."

HOU: "Roger, 2830 Lima. Lufkin altimeter
        29.94. Wind 180 at 10 knots. Lufkin
        elevation 654'. Good luck."

By this time, Bill was too busy to hear or
acknowledge the well-wishes. The Lufkin area of
Texas is called the Piney Woods for a reason—it is
almost total forest. Once before Bill had been lucky
enough to pull off an emergency landing at night and hit
an open field. The odds of that happening again were
almost nil.

With the full realization that within less than eight
minutes he would probably be dead, Bill began working
his emergency check list: ignition off—no sparks to
cause an explosion; fuel intake valve off; flaps
down—air speed down to minimum.

All this time the plane is moving toward the
ground at 900 feet a minute. Two minutes passed.

With visibility at zero, Bill knew he would never see the ground that would reach up to him.

Three minutes.   Bill helplessly watches the altimeter spiral downward through 3,000 feet.

At 2:53 p.m., one last call.

30L: "Lufkin radio.   2830 Lima.   I'm showing seven DME Lufkin VOR. 2,800 feet. No power."

LUFKIN: "Roger, 2830 Lima.   All traffic is cleared out. Lufkin altimeter 29.94. Good luck."

Bill is now two minutes from hitting something. What—he hasn't the faintest idea. At this moment, he realizes this is one time he is not in control, and he remembers Sue's new faith. Maybe now is a good time to try it.   In controlled panic, one prayer enters his mind.

"Please, God, give me another chance!"

2:55 p.m. Less than one minute from impact.

In such a situation, it is customary to land with the wheels up.   A belly landing is considered safer than a wheels-down landing. For some reason, just as Bill finished his prayer, he reached over and manually lowered the wheels.

Later, he could give no logical reason why he had done that. He just did. Thirty seconds later, in a fog so thick that one could see no more than five feet ahead, those lowered wheels touched down at the midway point of Runway 18 at Lufkin Airport. When the plane came to a stop, it was on the end of the runway just as though it had made a normal and scheduled landing.

There is an old story of a man who was working on a roof. He lost his balance and started to fall to the ground three stories below. In desperation he prayed, "Lord, help me!" About that time, a nail caught him and stopped his fall. Quickly he said, "Nevermind, Lord. I've got it under control."

Sitting on the end of a runway that was not supposed to be there, Bill Martin had no illusions. He was there, alive and unharmed, because Sue's God had heard his prayer and had found the runway that couldn't be seen with human eyes. Even before he got the door of the plane open, he thanked God for an answered prayer and pledged his life to His service.

The story finished, we sat looking at the mountain. We were back in the present, and Bill's church in Denton was raising money for a new Family Life Center.

After a few moments he said, "Ben, I don't know what we will give, but I do know this. God let me live for a purpose. I'm not here with you right now by accident. Let us pray about it, and sometime within the next week we will make our pledge."

I suppose a clever motivator or a godly hustler could have come up with a good guilt phrase to leave with him—something like, "Well, God let you live so I am sure He expects great things from you," or "After what He has done for you, you really owe God a lot. Looks like it's about time to settle the bill." You know, something really good to hook him into the program.

But, that is something I've just never been able to do. I've always worked on the premise that once the case has been presented, most of God's people are adult enough to make up their own minds without me trying to play God for them.

So I listened to Bill as he said that he would come by next week and make his pledge. I had no idea what it would be. I did know he was a person who knew the seriousness of his commitment to God. He was not playing games.

The following week, the pastor called me and told me that Bill and Sue had turned in their pledge along with a personal note to me. The note was sealed in an envelope, so it had not been opened.

When I got to the church that night, I hurried by the office to pick up the note. Inside was a handwritten note from Bill. It said, "Ben, thanks for coming out to Colorado and talking with Sue and me about the stewardship drive. It's always good to hear about things at the church, but I especially enjoyed swapping war stories with another pilot.

"Our pledge is for $126,734. I thought you might like to know how we arrived at the figure.

"After you left our mountain home last week, Sue and I sat and talked about what we have come to call 'The Landing at Lufkin.' You know, for me it all really started there. God so totally answered my prayer and so completely changed my life that somehow it seemed right that we tie our gift to His work to that event.

"Well, last week we pulled the invoice from the purchase of 2830 Lima. We paid exactly $126,734. Somehow it just seemed appropriate to give that amount back to Him."

▲ ▲ ▲
AN OBSERVATION
▼ ▼ ▼

I am a pilot with over 4,000 hours in my log book. There is nothing quite like the conversation carried on by pilots when they get together. Pilots are like fisherman. You can usually take what we say and divide it in half.

However, when a pilot has experienced extreme terror, the experience is usually psychologically ingrained forever. Several years ago I was flying my plane, in full instrument weather, across the Great Smokey Mountains when I realized that several of my basic instruments had gone out. The next 30 minutes were filled with an intensity I shall not long forget as I fought to get out of the clouds and land. Even today, when I tell the story, I feel the controlled panic all over again.

It was like that when I sat exchanging stories with Bill Martin. As Bill told of his emergency landing in East Texas, his hands began to shake and perspiration formed on his brow. He was living those awful hours all over again.

On the day that I read his note about their gift, I realized what Bill was doing. He was taking a very bad moment, an awful moment in his life, and reframing it with a good experience. I dare say, that in the future when Bill thinks of his failed engine experience, he will not focus so much on his proximity to death, but rather on his unusual opportunity in life.

People make their giving decisions in many ways and for many different reasons. Maybe someday I will cease to be amazed at the way people arrive at those giving decisions. Maybe someday I will cease to be amazed at how, in a single moment, God can answer a simple prayer and produce a runway out of the fog and rain.

Maybe someday . . . but I hope not.

CHAPTER VI

THE DISHWASHER

A s Ann Mitchell stood before the congregation of Calvary Church in Lexington, Kentucky, that morning, it was as though a lifetime of memories flashed before her. These were her people, and in a moment she was going to share with them one of the most personal decisions she had ever made. As she sat on the platform and looked at the 1,100 faces in the sanctuary, time stood still and memories paraded before her.

Some twenty years before as a twelve-year-old girl, she had walked forward in a morning service in this church to give her life to Christ. From that moment on, these people were not just impersonal individuals, they were family. For the next seven years, her junior high and high school years, these would be the people who would most influence and mold her life.

On the morning that she had gone forward to register her commitment to Christ, the first person by her side was Mrs. Thompson, her Sunday School teacher. Often she had sat in her living room and heard this godly woman talk about life, its purpose and its meaning. Perhaps it was here that she had first felt the longing to make her life count for something. Years later, Mrs. Thompson would not be one bit surprised when Ann Mitchell made the commitment to full-time Christian service.

Others influenced her during this time. Dr. Fuller was more than just her pastor, he was a friend. That summer at church youth camp when she had sat under a big oak tree trying to put it all together, it was Dr. Fuller who had taken the time to reassure her that God did indeed have a place for her in His great plan, and in time He would reveal it. No pressure, no guilt, no unnecessary emotion, but rather the calm, simple reassurance that in time it would all work out for her.

In the life of most churches, there is that period of time that is filled with a unique group of young people. It is a time that older people look back on and say such things as, "You remember, it was when Ann Mitchell and all of that group was in junior high."

Well, Ann's school years were like that for her and the people at Calvary. So many from that youth group gave their lives for special service. Joe Newberry, mischievous to a fault, turned out to be an associate pastor of one of the largest churches in Louisville. Ann's best friend, Delain Forest, went on to medical school and is now a medical staff member on the USS Hope. Bill Barton, perhaps Ann's first love, as well as the first love of practically every other girl in school, had surrendered to the ministry, but was killed in a hunting accident during his third year in college.

But you see the pattern. In that group of young people, there was a sense of mission, of selflessness, of calling to serve. And one by one, they answered that inward call to service. When the final total was in, there were seventeen people who made up that "group of kids" at Calvary, and nine of them had made a commitment to some kind of Christian service.

Ann Mitchell was a senior in high school when she went forward to publicly commit her life to missions. No one was particularly surprised. This was the group of kids who were serious about life. They would be remembered and supported and loved by this church for a long time.

After high school, Ann went to college to prepare for whatever it might be that God had in store for her. The months passed all too quickly. She was extremely popular in college. With studies and social activities and church, her life was moving at an unbelievable pace. Because of this, the call from Bob Brightman asking her to go with him to the Arkansas football game made no important impact on her. This was just another date with another guy whom she had, no doubt, met somewhere on campus.

The football game was okay, but the date was one to remember. Bob turned out to be a law student she had met earlier at a group discussion on world conflicts. She had been impressed with him at the time, but it was not until he came to the dorm to pick her up that she placed a face with the name.

As they sat over dinner that night and discussed the future, Ann felt the security to open her dreams and sense of mission. Bob not only understood, but shared his own commitment to Christ and to Christian service. Six weeks later, they were pinned. Three months later, they were engaged. And one year later to the day, they walked down the center aisle of Calvary Church to hear Dr. Fuller pronounce them husband and wife.

Back to school for their senior year and back to Lexington for the Christmas holidays, it was at that time that Bob and Ann once again came before the church to tell the people of their commitment to missions. They asked the church's blessings as they finished their college work and entered the seminary to prepare for a life of service in foreign missions.

Three years later, they completed their seminary work, and at the same time, finalized their request for an appointment to South America as missionaries. In July of 1979, Bob and Ann Brightman stood once again before the congregation at Calvary accepting the prayers and best wishes as they departed for their first tour of duty in the mountains of Chile, South America. It would be five long, hard years before they would be with these people—their people—again.

To describe those years as difficult would be an understatement. The first year in Chili, they both struggled with the language and all the adjustments to a new culture. That first year was spent in Santiago, the capital city, but it was probably more difficult than the next four years which were spent in the smaller villages along the Bioblo River, because in that first year, Ann was pregnant with their first child. Combine that with the homesickness and health problems they suffered, and it is easy to see how the year could be considered difficult.

After language school, they were sent to Los Creaos, a town of 24,000 people in the central part of the country, to begin work with a new fellowship of believers. The third year, the mission sent them to Del Rios, a village of 6,400 people in the mountain region of central Chile, to work in the development of a new school. The fourth and fifth years, they were assigned to a rural village of less than 1,000 population to help start a literacy program.

Some nights as they came to the end of another strenuous day, Ann would joke with Bob and say that one more move and they would be living alone. It seemed that with each move, life became more difficult.

At the end of the fifth year, they were scheduled to return home to the United States for a year's sabbatical. It could not have come at a better time. Their second child had been born the year before and with that there was an even greater responsibility. Both Ann and Bob were ready to come home. Their commitment to the mission was no less—they would be ready to return in time, but right now they were tired. Lexington, Kentucky, seemed like a long way off, but if they could get there, it would be heaven.

On April 13, 1984, they boarded a plane in Santiago, Chile, bound for Houston. From there, they would fly home. A man, a woman, a four-year-old girl, and a one-year-old baby all boarded the plane that day. It was good to be going home!

Just before leaving, Bishop Robert Willis, Administrator of the South American mission, had called Bob to his office. There were tears in his eyes as he spoke. "Bob," he began, "how can I ever thank you for the sacrifices that you and Ann have made this year? In all of my 22 years in Chile, I have never asked one of our new couples to serve in so many difficult places. And, I might add, I have never seen a couple so readily accept the mission assigned them.

"When I sent you to that last assignment, I knew that I was asking you to accept a difficult position. You never questioned or complained. For that, I want to thank you. It is evident that God put you here. It is also evident that the two of you have earned the rest this year will bring you.

"But before you go, I want you to know where your assignment will be upon your return. The Christian Mission College in Santiago will need a new president next year. Upon your return, I would like to submit your name for that position. I think it is time for you and Ann to have an easier place of service. With your permission, I'll see that the position is yours upon your return."

There was no way to adequately describe the next moment. Put simply, Bob cried. For five years he had watched Ann grow old. At 28, she looked 40. He had seen her cook on a wood stove at their last assignment. He had watched her washing diapers by hand day after

day because of the lack of any type of modern facilities.
He had kissed her goodbye as she got in a jeep with a
native driver to take the baby 60 miles over a dirt road
to see a doctor. All without complaint.

"Oh, dear God, thank you. It is going to be
better for Ann." For that gift, Bob cried.

And back at the hotel when he told Ann, she
cried, too. Only then did they truly understand the
price that they had paid over the past five years. They
were on their way home for a year of study and rest.
But when they returned, it would be to a city, to a real
home, to a school for the children, and to a grocery
store, and to a mission position at the college where
both of them could make a real impact on the outreach
into Chile. They laughed, they cried, and then they
boarded a plane for Lexington, Kentucky.

Somewhere over the Gulf of Mexico, Ann raised
her head from Bob's shoulder and whispered in his ear,
"A dishwasher."

Without opening his eyes, Bob replied, "What?
What did you say?"

"A dishwasher. That's what I want to bring back
next year. I want a dishwasher in our new home. We
can't afford to buy one down here, so I'll bring it back
with us." Then, with a chuckle in her voice, "I don't
want much, just a dishwasher. See how easy I am to
please!" And she slipped back into sleep.

A quick change of planes in Houston and two hours later the Brightmans were sharing tears of joy with their family in Lexington. A much needed year of rest and renewal was beginning.

During the year, they would live in a special missionary home provided by Calvary Church. Bob worked on staff at Calvary and Ann enjoyed having the children in a place with family so near. She was able to play the role of full-time mother and wife, a role that she had not often enjoyed in her life with Bob.

They had been home for about two months when Dr. Fuller announced a major building program for Calvary Church. Immediately following that announcement, there was a kick-off for a drive to raise the money for the new facility. Bob and Ann had been surprised to learn on their arrival back at the church, that in their absence, growth in church membership had been substantial. The church sanctuary seated 1,100 people, and it was filled to capacity for three Sunday morning services.

A new facility with a cost in excess of $3 million would be needed to meet the growing needs of the church. Surely to accomplish that would require unusual sacrifice from everyone. The program was launched and the next few months would tell its effectiveness.

One evening after church services, Ann and Bob sat down to discuss their participation. No doubt there were those in the congregation who would feel they had already sacrificed enough for the cause, but that was not their philosophy. Somehow they felt that Calvary was their church for this year, and their "home" church no matter where they were. They wanted to be a part of its growth and future.

After careful consideration and intense calculation of their resources, they mutually agreed on their participation in the program. Even though two-and-one-half years of the three-year pledge period would find them back in Chile, they still agreed to make a three-year pledge. When they shared their decision with their friend and pastor, Dr. Fuller, he was overwhelmed.

He, like many of the congregation, was well aware of the sacrifices Bob and Ann had already made. He neither expected more from them nor encouraged their participation. Their decision was a special blessing for him, and he asked them to share their decision with the congregation on Sunday morning. Bob deferred to Ann, and on the last Sunday of the program, she stood before the congregation to share their decision.

"I have never really known what it means to sacrifice," she began, "but from the moment Bob and I first heard about this program, we wanted to do something that would be a sacrifice to us. Something that would cost us. Something that we couldn't do on our own without it really affecting our lifestyle.

"Two weeks ago, we decided to make a commitment of $25 per month. That will not be extremely difficult while we are here in the States, but beginning in about five months, it will really touch us deeply. That is what our family has decided to do, and I wanted to share with you that, at our house, that was a good decision."

And then she paused. Everyone waited to see what was coming next, and when nothing was said Dr. Fuller started to rise and walk to the pulpit. As he did, Ann turned and asked him for just one other word.

"Last night, as I was preparing for this morning, I was faced with the fact that sacrifice is never collective. At some point, for it to be sacrifice, it must be intensely personal. Our $25 a month commitment is a family commitment. Somehow, I personally needed to do something for me.

"When I came home this year, I had a personal goal. I wanted to buy a dishwasher and take it back to the mission field with us. For the first time in six years, our family will have a home that is somewhat permanent. I know it sounds trivial, but it is something that I have planned and wanted for a long time. I hoped for a dishwasher.

"So I've saved the $600 that it will cost to buy and equip the dishwasher for installation in Chile. I've made arrangements for a manufacturer to ship the unit for us. But last night, I decided the dishwasher will be my personal sacrifice. Over and above our family commitment, I am giving the $600 that I had saved for the dishwasher."

Throughout the congregation—silence. And in the silence, she continued, "Now I have one other thing to say to you good people here at Calvary. You are such giving people that I know what is going to happen. After this service, someone is going to come up to me and tell me not to worry about it, that you are going to give me a dishwasher to take home to Chile.

"Hear me now. Please don't do that. Please don't take away my sacrifice. For the next five years, I want to stand at my sink in our home in Chile and wash my dishes and thank God for the people and ministry of Calvary Church. Please don't take my sacrifice away from me."

▲ ▲ ▲
AN OBSERVATION
▼ ▼ ▼

Over the years I have watched thousands of people go through the giving process. How well I know that there is a biblical principle involved in "sowing and reaping," but when I first met Ann Brightman, I was impressed by the fact that this woman had that biblical concept in the proper perspective.

It was clear to me that she understood the biblical concept of giving when she said, "Please don't take my sacrifice away from me."

How many times do each of us come to the giving process with the hidden hope that somehow God will make it up to us in kind? That somehow, we really will not have to give at all. We will simply make a deposit with God and wait for Him to do His thing for us as a reward.

I remember a few years ago when I was working a program in New England, seeing a young businessman go through the giving process. It was especially interesting because this young man spent hours with me talking about his concept of giving.

He used cliché phrases such as "You can't outgive God," and "It always comes back a thousand times." Now I knew where he was coming from when he talked like that. Yet, I really did not understand how very far this philosophy had influenced his thinking until one night after a service we sat at my hotel and talked over a late night snack.

As we talked that night, he said, "Ben, I'm going to tell you something that no one else knows. My business is almost at the point of bankruptcy. Just before coming over tonight, I called my accountant and he tells me, that as of today, I have less than $7,500 in the bank. Well, I have decided to give it all because if I do, I believe that God is honor-bound to pull my business out of bankruptcy."

I tried to explain that is not necessarily the way it works, but I never did get through. You just do not bargain with God like that. That's shallow, unbiblical, and degrading to the person of God.

All of my reasoning failed, and a few days later, with a great deal of boasting, he walked forward at the close of the service and publicly demanded that God take his money. I was not there that morning, but I am told that he almost dared God not to "honor" his gift. It was reported that he stood before the congregation and boldly stated, "I am giving God my last $7,000. Publicly, I challenge you to see what God does with my business."

About eight months later, I was back in that town to make a follow-up visit to the church. While talking with the pastor, he informed me of the end to the story.

Less than two months after the program closed, that man's business went under. He lost his business, his home, his car, and the pastor said that his marriage was coming apart. He had grown bitter blaming God for all of his troubles. He no longer bothered to come to church.

Sad. How very sad.

I contrast that with one who says, "I am giving my dishwasher. Don't give me another one. Please don't take my sacrifice away from me."

Now, you tell me: who is more clearly setting the example of Christ-like giving?

CHAPTER VII

ADVICE

A dvice. Everyone gives it. Most people don't like to accept it, and few people follow it. But as Debbie Sandel sat in the doctor's office that Thursday morning, she knew if everything turned out as she expected, she was in for a lot of it.

She was shaken from her thoughts by the call of her name instructing her to Examination Room #3. She had never been here before and the surroundings were new and foreign. Everything seemed so cold and forbidding as she entered the room. The nurse told her the doctor would be in shortly.

Dr. Rogers had been her family doctor since high school, but she just could not go to him this time. He was more than a family doctor, he was a close family friend. Dr. Rogers and her father played golf once a week, and every Sunday the two families worshipped at the same church. Her last year in high school, their families had even taken a vacation to Canada together. No, this time she simply could not face Dr. Rogers. This time she needed anonymity, not a family friend.

A lifetime of moments passed before the doctor, this unknown doctor in this unknown clinic, entered the room. A brief discussion, an impersonal examination, and instructions to get dressed and meet him in his office in five minutes. Five minutes away from the news that she dreaded with every cell of her being.

"Debbie," he began, "you are about eight weeks pregnant."

Then came the list of things to do and not do, the instruction to make another appointment in four weeks, and the meaningless congratulations spoken with the same blandness as everything else had been spoken. Through the foggy haze of confusion, she listened and tried to accept what was being said.

She was sitting in her car at a traffic light at the corner of Speight Avenue and Eighth Street when the reality of it all began to hit home. And when it did, the tears came like a storm. Only the insistent blowing of car horns prodded her on toward her apartment and the reality of her situation.

She was twenty-three years old and one year out of college. She had taken a job as a legal secretary for a large law firm, and she had been dating one of the partners in the firm for about six months. He was young, ambitious, single, and exciting. She was to find out later that he was also selfish, uncaring, and a people-user.

On the night before her visit to the unknown doctor, she had invited him over to her apartment. After a nice meal over wine and candlelight, she explained to him that she thought she was pregnant.

She wasn't sure how she had expected him to act, but his reaction caught her totally by surprise.

Accusations, threats, anger, disgust, disapproval— all came into play. He was taking the same defensive position he might use in a legal case. It was as though she had planned this to trap him into marriage. She had never seen such panic and hate fill the face of anyone—a face of not loving, not caring. He had professed love for her. When he walked out the door, she found out how alone loneliness could be.

Two days later, still trying to face the reality of it all, she was called into the manager's office and told that the firm was cutting back on staff. Her job was terminated. No, there was no reason to stay through the rest of the day. They would mail her final check to her. Yes, they would give her a good reference. There was no mention of a young partner in the firm who may have recommended her termination.

From that point forward, she never heard from or approached the baby's father. From that point forward, the decisions would be hers alone.

Debbie spent the next few days taking care of the immediate problems. There were several. First, she had to get a job. With her qualifications, that came surprisingly easy, and within a week she was working for another law firm only blocks away from her previous employer. True to his word, her former manager had put in an excellent word of recommendation. At least that portion of her life was stable again.

The next decision was the most difficult one that she would ever face in her life. As Debbie saw it, there were three options available to her. First, there was always the abortion option. Several of her friends had taken that route, and it was certainly one that she would want to explore. Second, she could have the baby and adopt it out after birth. Finally, she could have the baby and raise it as a single parent. Debbie found that listing options on paper was infinitely easier than making the final decision.

The first logical step seemed to be a talk with her parents. While they had never been a very close family, they were still family and would want the best for her.

"Oh, my God, how could you do this to me! How the hell do you expect me to face my bridge club, my friends, when my daughter is living like a tramp?"

From the moment her mother screamed those words, Debbie blanked out everything else. The tirade continued, but went unheard. Her father sat with his head down, not looking at her, and after a few minutes, he just got up and walked from the room. And on and on her mother went. Finally, with her mother in tears, Debbie got up, walked across the room, and tried to put her arms around this woman who seemed to be in such agony. When she felt her mother pull away and when she saw the look of disgust on her face, Debbie felt the loneliness close in around her all over again. Putting on her coat, she walked to the door with the realization that a tie had been broken that perhaps would never again be mended.

That night, for the very first time, she seriously considered abortion. A call to a friend and she had the name of a local clinic. An appointment the next day indicated that if the procedure was to be carried out, it would have to be within the next six weeks. At that moment, the clock started ticking on the decision that would soon be forced.

Debbie had never really been a religious person, so for her there was no great theological conflict. In her mind, it was more a practical matter than a theological one. It was not until she was having a coffee break one day with Gail Jordon, a new friend at work, that the religious factor came into the equation. And even then, it was a casual intrusion, not forced.

Gail was a member of a singles group at Trinity Lutheran Church. That night, they were having a think tank discussion on the problems and opportunities of being single in a modern world. When she invited Debbie to be a part of the discussion, she neither knew Debbie's situation nor the specific topic of discussion for the evening session.

Having nothing else to do and needing to get her mind off her troubles, Debbie agreed to go. They met for a snack before the meeting and arrived at the church just as the session was beginning.

As the leader began talking to the group of about thirty people, Debbie looked around to see who attended such gatherings. They seemed to be average people, mostly around her age, a good mix of men and women, fairly intelligent, and very comfortable with one another. She got the impression that most of them knew at least part of the group. There was a casual atmosphere, as even during the opening remarks, some got up to get a cup of coffee or to say hello to a late comer.

The general remarks were over and the speaker was announcing the topic for the evening. "One of the ethical areas facing many young people today is the subject of abortion. Tonight, I would like for us to explore that subject from the Christian perspective."

For the next hour a practical debate raged, as one by one, speaker after speaker, shared their views. Debbie was amazed at the frankness and openness of the discussion. One girl said that she had an abortion as a teenager, and she shared the hurt and guilt that she still felt.

A young guy told of the abortion that his girlfriend had and how he had been no part of that decision. Even now as he talked, one could feel the sadness. The openness of the discussion totally overwhelmed Debbie. Here were people her own age grappling with the "right and wrong" of an issue that, at this very moment, was very real to her.

Just before the meeting closed, one of the pastors, Tom Reeves, and his wife, Becky, shared their personal story. Four years earlier, their only son had been killed by a hit-and-run driver. They talked about Jimmy and his five years of life that had ended in such a tragic way. Finally, through tears, Becky made this emotional plea. "Tom and I lost our son four years ago. We will never get over that tragic day in our lives. Even more tragic for us is the fact that we can never have any more children. The two of us have so much love to share, and yet, we can never have a child of our own again.

"So here is my plea to you tonight. Someday, someone you know may face this issue of abortion in a very personal way. My plea is that if they do, and if you can have any input into their decision, please, please ask them to consider adoption instead. There are thousands of us out there who would love to give a baby a warm, loving, and caring home."

Whether she agreed with the speakers or not, Debbie had to admit that she was leaving the meeting that night with a lot to think about.

Tom Reeves had been minister of the singles group at Trinity Lutheran for three years. Those who knew him knew that his normal clerical garb consisted of blue jeans, sweat shirts, and tennis shoes. His approach to ministry was just as casual. When he called Debbie the following week to make an appointment to visit with her, it was a natural follow-up to the singles discussion group she had attended the previous week.

Two days later, sitting over a cup of coffee at the Lazy Tiger coffee house around the corner from her apartment, Debbie found Tom to be the most open person she had ever met. There was no pretense about him. He had asked for the visit simply to say how pleased they would be to have her in the church singles group on a permanent basis.

How it happened she might never remember, but before the second cup of coffee, Debbie was laying bare her soul to this minister who seemed to understand what life was all about. He listened, he cared, he seemed to understand, and most of all, he didn't moralize or preach.

Quietly, he shared his feelings. "From a personal viewpoint, I don't believe in abortion. For me, it is morally wrong. But Debbie, I can't make the decision for you. It is something that you must struggle with until you are at peace—at peace with what I would call 'God's will for your life in this matter,' but what you might, at this point, simply view as peace within your own being.

"But, I want you to know this. I care and I represent a God who cares and I represent a people who care. If you will allow us to, we will love you through this decision until you come to know His will."

Two words spoken over a cup of coffee at a neighborhood cafe made a significant impact on her life. Oh, how ready Debbie was to hear someone say "I care."

That night, Debbie came to two decisions. The first decision was that the option of abortion was not a valid option for her. Again, not for moral reasons, but simply because she did not think she could handle the psychology of it. She eliminated that option. What a tremendous relief that was. The second decision was to get to know more about the people at Trinity Lutheran. Right now, she needed someone to care. If they were at all like Tom and Becky, then maybe that was where she needed to be.

Now she was down to two options. Would she give the baby up for adoption or keep the child to raise on her own? She might be down to two options, but they certainly were not getting any easier.

For the next few months, Debbie attended the singles group at Trinity Lutheran every week. She found herself surrounded by people who accepted her and her situation without being judgmental. Frankly, she found it rather astounding that over those weeks, never once did anyone tell her what she "ought" to be doing. In quiet, simple ways, they let her know that she was accepted and that they would accept her decision about her circumstances as a private matter; their decision to support, not theirs to make.

Over the next couple of months, Debbie found herself getting more involved at Trinity Lutheran than she might ever have expected. Her friendship with Tom and Becky Reeves grew rapidly. Evenings together were spent talking about everything from religion to pop rock artists. They played Scrabble and made posters for the children's play at church. What they did not do was talk about a subject that Becky had wanted to bring up a thousand times.

So many times she wanted to let Debbie know again that if she wanted to have a good home for her baby, she and Tom would be willing to provide that home. Her own heart ached for a child, and she knew that Tom felt the same way. But never once did she cross that unspoken line of trust. Any decision made would have to be made by Debbie without pressure or input from her.

I am not certain when the decision was made. Perhaps there was not a specific time that could be marked on the calendar. But the decision was shared with Tom and Becky one evening after the singles group meeting at the church. Debbie had asked if she could come by for a cup of coffee, and of course, the invitation was immediately extended.

Realizing that something was on her mind, no one pressed for conversation. After a few minutes, Debbie spoke. "Before I tell you why I wanted to come by tonight, I want to say something that I don't know exactly how to put in words. Thank you doesn't seem exactly right, but right now, it's the best I can do.

"Over these past few months, the two of you have been such an important part of my life. Tom, when you said to me at the Lazy Tiger that you cared about me, it was like water to a thirsty traveller. How badly I needed someone to care that day. For that, I am so grateful to you.

"Introduction to the singles group was just the right thing at exactly the right time. How you ever put together such a great group of people, I'll never know. But you did, and I thank you for letting me be a part of it.

"Becky, that first night, when you shared your story during the discussion on abortion, it was a real eye-opener for me. Thank you for being that open. If you could only know how much I needed that kind of openness. In a few minutes, you taught me that this group could be trusted. I needed to trust. Thank you so much.

"I wish I could tell you how much I love you both.

"Yesterday, or perhaps last night—I'm not sure exactly when I came to the decision—but I've decided to keep the baby. I know it won't be easy being a single parent, but for me, it's right. No one that I know will understand the decision except you and the group. I'll need your support."

For each of us, there are a few special moments in life that are recorded forever. For the next few minutes, Tom, Becky, and Debbie shared a few of those moments. They held each other and shared each other's tears. Tears of joy, of love, of happiness, of disappointment, and of friendship.

Five months later, at 2:35 in the morning, Sara Gail Sandel was born. Tom and Becky were present to share the event. They were also there two days later when Debbie took her six-and-one-half pound baby home to begin their life together.

Sara Gail was almost four years old when I first met her and heard Debbie's story and the decision she had made. We had been retained to assist Trinity

Lutheran in raising money for a new family counseling center.

When Tom Reeves introduced Debbie to me, I knew nothing about her background or the decision that she had made. Since she was working with the abortion counseling group, I did not get to know her over the months that we worked on the fund drive.

One night after a session, a few of us went over to Tom and Becky's home for a time of fellowship. After everyone else had gone and just the Reeves, Debbie, and I remained, Tom indicated that Debbie had something she wanted to share with me. Motioning me into the bedroom, Debbie pointed out the most beautiful little blond-haired girl that I have ever seen. Quietly, without waking her, Debbie kissed her and then we moved back to the living room.

"Ben," she began, "that little girl is in my life today because of the people at Trinity Lutheran. After she was born, I became a member there and now I want to provide a place of help for others like me. I don't have much. I work as a legal secretary, and child care alone eats up most of my salary.

"But this is important to me. I've been thinking about it and if I pass up my IRA contribution for the next three years, I can give that $6,000 to the fund drive for the counseling center. Right now, that seems more important to me. Please add that amount to the pledge total."

When I got back to the hotel that night, I did a quick calculation. Debbie was twenty-eight years old. She was giving up three years of investment to her IRA that would have been her retirement at age sixty-five. Assuming a normal rate of interest, her $6,000 gift had cost her over $120,000.

Would she have given it if she had taken time to run the same calculation that I did? After seeing little Sara Gail and hearing her mother's story, I think that she would.

▲ ▲ ▲
AN OBSERVATION
▼ ▼ ▼

Today there is a new counseling center at Trinity Lutheran Church. All types of problems and opportunities are dealt with by the professional staff. The center is managed by a five-person lay committee charged with the responsibility of managing and administering the center. Debbie Sandel is the chairperson of that committee.

CHAPTER VIII

THE BEST-LAID PLANS

A few months ago I had been asked to speak at an advance commitment dinner in Charlotte, North Carolina. On such occasions, we will often gather a few of the church leaders together in a home to discuss the options available for making commitments to the program. We may discuss real estate or stock transfers or other types of gifts-in-kind; a gift-in-kind being anything of value other than money.

Obviously, when such topics are discussed, you open the program to the receipt of junk gifts. There are always people who want to get rid of their 1973 Fords with no engines and get a tax write-off. But, I always figure that is their problem, not mine. So I usually challenge people to look for ways to increase their giving through gifts-in-kind.

After the meeting that evening, I had returned to my hotel and gone to bed. Now sleep does not come easily to me, but when it does, I tend to awaken slowly. On some days I may be out of bed for an hour or two before the world comes into focus.

So on this evening when the phone rang, I assumed it was my wake-up call, and only as I reached to answer it did I notice that it was 12:15 in the morning. Jumping to the conclusion that something terrible had happened, I was brought immediately awake as I answered the phone.

"Ben, I'm so sorry to call this late. Were you asleep?"

"Of course not," I mumbled. I was just sitting around waiting for your call, I thought, but didn't say.

"Ben, this is Herb Rollins. My wife Fran and I were at the dinner at the Webb's house tonight. At that dinner, you asked each of us to begin praying to know God's will about our commitment to the new sanctuary. You said that some of us would have an answer to that prayer before we got home tonight while others would struggle for weeks to find His will.

"Well, Ben, we have the answer and we just have to share it with you. We are in the lobby of the hotel right now. Would you mind meeting us in the coffee shop and letting us tell you about it?"

By this time, I am awake. The odds of going back to sleep are slim. I have a 6:00 a.m. flight and they are in the lobby. "Fine," I said, "let's have a cup of coffee."

Over the next forty minutes, this is the story I heard.

"Tonight, before we left the Webb's, we prayed that God would show us what He wanted to do through us. We didn't know whether that answer would come tomorrow or next month, but we prayed that we would accept His leadership in this decision.

"On the way home, we stopped at the Quick-Stop for milk. Fran stayed in the car and I went in to buy the milk. When I opened the door to get back in the car, it hit me. I knew what our decision must be. As I got in, I told Fran that I had an answer. Before I could say anything else, she said, "It's the house, isn't it?"

"I almost fainted, Ben, because that was exactly what I was thinking."

Fran picked up the story. "You see, we were married seven years ago. When we got married, we immediately bought our present home and financed it on a seven-year mortgage. Both of us are CPAs, and we make pretty good salaries. There are no children in our plans, so we sort of had a dream house as our focus.

"Two years ago, we bought a double lot out at the lake. Our plan has been to pay off our present home—it will be paid off in three months—and then sell it and build our dream home at the lake."

Herb's turn. "Ben, if you came over to our house right now you would see on the den wall the architect's drawing of our dream home. It fits perfectly on our lot. Our plan was to put our house on the market next month and then start building the new one immediately."

Fran again. "Sitting in the parking lot at the Quick-Stop tonight, we talked about it. We talked about selling our current house, it's worth about $90,000, and giving that toward the new sanctuary. Then we went home and looked at the drawing again. We cried a little until around midnight, but we were at peace that this was the right decision."

Herb reached over and put his hand on Fran's before he closed the discussion by saying, "You know, Ben, the more we talked about it the more we decided that we have a lifetime to build our house. But we may never again have an opportunity to build a house for God."

▲ ▲ ▲

AN OBSERVATION

▼ ▼ ▼

Let me share a couple of thoughts with you. John Ruskin once said, "Everywhere I have ever worshipped was built by someone else. And now it is my time." Perhaps for Herb and Fran, it was their time.

Recently another couple in another city in another church made a similar decision. They summed it up by saying, "Suddenly we realized that our dream house seated 3,000 people."

CHAPTER IX

THE FISHERMAN

I f you don't like to fish, you may want to skip this story. First of all, you won't understand the depth of the sacrifice, and secondly, you probably won't care. Those who fish are a breed unto themselves, and this is the story of a fisherman.

My stepfather used to say that he never knew a fisherman who was not "shiftless, worthless, lazy, and good for nothing." My stepfather was a fisherman.

My mother used to say that "a fisherman's wife was neglected on Saturday afternoon, lied to on Saturday night about how many fish were caught, and always expected to be happy about having to cook the dumb fish." My mother was a fisherman's wife.

Now, let me introduce you to Jake. Jake had a last name, but few people knew what it was, and if I told you, you would forget, too, so let's not waste our time. Just remember that Jake was, and is, a fisherman. I am going to tell you a good deal more about Jake, but to keep everything in perspective, you have to remember that the first passion in his life was fishing.

Jake made his living as a delivery man with the United States Postal Service. He had walked his route in San Antonio, Texas, for almost thirty-five years. Jake was married to a woman named Lettie. They had been married for more years than either of them cared to remember, but for those thirty-five years that Jake had worked for the post office, Lettie had made his lunch and sent him on his way every workday morning come rain or shine.

If you asked Jake what he did, he would say that he was a postman. If you asked Lettie what Jake did, she would say he was a fisherman. I guess it is all in the point of view. Both were looking at it from the viewpoint of thirty-five years of marriage.

Jake had learned to fish at his father's knee. His father had never been much for work, so at every opportunity he would take up the cane pole and head for the lake. Little Jake would grab a cane and trudge along with him. His father was a great storyteller (but what fisherman isn't) and would spend the afternoon spinning yarns to his little son. Some days they actually caught a fish.

It was during those years with his father that Jake learned that there was more to life than working. Never one to have an extra dollar to his name, his father still seemed to have enough to get by. They were never very hungry, they stayed warm in the winter, and they spent a lot of time fishing. All in all, it didn't seem to be a bad deal—as far as Jake was concerned.

When Jake was twenty-years old, he went to work
for the U.S. Postal Service, married Lettie, and caught
the largest big-mouth bass that most people in that area
had ever seen.   If you asked him what route he covered
on his first day on the job, Jake wouldn't have the
foggiest idea.   If you were so bold as to ask him the
color of the dress that Lettie had been wearing as they
stood before the Justice of the Peace in Hood County,
he would look at you like you had lost your mind.

But, for the record, he would say he caught that
big-mouth bass on a white-feather, belly-flopper top
water lure.   It was on a four-pound test line, and he
was just a few miles short of the three-mile marker up
on Hodges Lake.   It was about 3:30 in the afternoon
and the sun had been behind the clouds all day.   He
caught about fifteen other fish on that same day, but not
one of them could match that big-mouth bass.

So, it was not as though Jake had a bad memory.
It was just rather selective.

Now, Jake was not selfish about his fishing.   He
would take Lettie anytime she wanted to go.   Every
weekend as he would leave to go to the lake, he would
invite her to go with him.   Sometimes she did, and
sometimes she didn't.   She could take it or leave it,
which I suppose says something about her commitment
to the vocation.

Every year when they planned their two weeks of
vacation, Jake tried to make certain that the lake they
went to had a good sightseeing area close by just in
case Lettie decided she wanted to do something besides

fish. He couldn't imagine such a thing, but from time to time it happened. When it did, he liked for her to have some place to go while he "drowned the worm," as he said. So, as you can see, Jake was not one bit selfish about this business of fishing.

For Christmas of 1964, he even gave Lettie a genuine Flex-Rite rod and a Blue Diamond reel. He had personally been hinting for that rod and reel set all year. She gave him a new stainless steel, lifetime guaranteed fish cleaning knife. Yep, '64 was a good Christmas.

Keep in mind that this was the pattern of their life together for thirty-five years. There was probably no gift exchanged, no vacation planned, no weekend spent together or apart that did not in some way show the influence of the quest for fish.

I know it's evident by now, but let me repeat. Jake was a fisherman and Lettie was a fisherman's wife.

They were camping and fishing up in Big Lake bottom in the summer of 1977 when they were first introduced to the inside of a new Comfort Ease Travel Trailer. It happened this way....

When Jake and Lettie camped, they camped. None of that life of ease for them. They had a friend who said his idea of roughing it was to be in a Holiday Inn with the TV broken, but that was not the way Jake and Lettie approached camping. When they camped, they camped!

They had a two-person tent and a full set of Coleman cooking equipment. They only got the Coleman stove after they spent three days in the backwoods of Colorado without a fire because all the wood was wet and wouldn't burn. Lettie threatened to stay home on the next trip if Jake didn't get a stove. Knowing exactly how far he could push, Jake bought a stove.

On this particular trip to Big Lake, they had been in their tent for three days and nights when, upon returning to camp after a hard day of fishing, they saw in the next campsite a new Comfort Ease Travel Trailer. There it sat in all of its glorious splendor. Lettie immediately saw that it had running water and a rest room. Jake sort of noticed the built-in rod carrier on the undercarriage.

Before long, they were knocking on the door to meet the owners of this luxurious camping machine, and not long after that, they were sitting in the kitchen area drinking hot coffee and dreading going back to their tent.

Jake had made a surprising discovery. He learned that the owner of this penthouse-on-wheels was as avid a fisherman as he was, thus dispelling the myth that only "wimps and city folks" would ever go to the lake in a rolling hotel.

They talked about the trailer all the way back to San Antonio. Lettie liked the fact that, after a long day of fishing, you could come in and take a hot bath. She liked the fact that on a cold, rainy weekend such as the one they had just experienced, she could actually sleep in a warm bed rather than a sleeping bag. Maybe she could even stay in bed while Jake got up at the crack of dawn to go fishing.

Jake liked the storage area in the rear that was large enough to hold all of his equipment without having to box and pack it after each trip. He liked the way you could put travel stickers on the rear end showing all of the places they had visited. He could envision a sign on the back that said something like, "Goin' Fishing and Ain't Coming Back."

In a nutshell, Lettie and Jake were hooked. From that trip on, they planned the day when they could buy a travel trailer. The Comfort Ease was high on their list.

Never one to do things halfway, Jake studied every possible option available to a serious fisherman looking for a trailer. He visited showrooms and brought home brochures. He compared prices of every model, both new and used. He spent hours with his calculator figuring out how the trailer could be bought and paid for by the time he retired. But don't dismay. While he was doing all this, there was never a weekend he was not at the lake looking to top the last record catch.

Finally, he sat down with Lettie one night and set out his plan. He was fifty-eight years old. If they set aside $338.34 each payday until he was sixty-two, they could pay cash for a new Comfort Ease Trailer, Model

#2189. That was the one with the extra storage space for fishing equipment.

By taking retirement from his job at age sixty-two, they would then have a trailer that was paid for and a retirement income that would allow them the freedom to travel and fish 365 days a year if they so desired. Jake didn't know a lot about heaven, but he thought that would have to be close to what God had in mind.

With that game plan before them, the first deposit was made to the "Trailer Fund" on March 1, 1984. The game plan to heaven was underway. It would be impossible to describe the excitement that was involved in making that deposit.

For the next three years and eight months, not one single deposit was missed. On November 1, 1987, Jake applied for early retirement. When approval came through, a process that took about six months, Jake and Lettie would be free to travel and fish, or as Jake would put it, "fish and travel."

Jake and Lettie were not what you would call "religious types." They were members of an independent Baptist church in San Antonio, Texas, but more so in name than in commitment. In fact, had the transmission in their Blazer not been acting up this particular weekend, they would have been at the lake and not sitting in a worship service at church.

The moment Jake looked at the bulletin, he wished he had stayed home. Obviously, the church was in some sort of building program, and it looked like the whole service was going to be a pitch for money. There was a testimony about giving and the sermon topic was "Ground Zero—A Starting Point." Jake had no idea what that meant, but he was convinced it had to do with getting his money.

Oh well, it was too late now, so he might as well sit back and get it over with.

As the service progressed, several facts became evident to Jake. First of all, the church was going to build a new sanctuary. Jake thought, "God knows we need one. If this old lady sittin' next to me weighed one more pound, she'd be sittin' in my lap."

Next he learned this was the second week in a four-week emphasis to "get the message out about the program to raise the money for the building." Well, you can't win them all, and it was just blind luck that this was the week that the transmission went out in the Blazer.

Finally, he understood that someone was encouraging people to "just find the will of God about this business of giving." He had no idea what that meant, but as Miss Betty Johnson stood to give her testimony, he began to get the picture.

Miss Betty was sixty-two, the same age as Jake, and a widow. No one could remember when her husband had died, so the title "Miss" just seemed to fit. As she stood that morning, she said she had come to the stewardship program convinced that she should be against it. She related how she had been afraid that someone was going to pressure her to give. Then, she said, she began to understand that the only thing that she would be asked to do was seek to know the will of God about this matter in her life.

She talked about that process, and how after a lot of prayer and a lot of soul-searching, she had decided to give up a cruise she had saved for and dreamed about for years. The $3,000 that she was going to spend on that cruise she was now giving to the building program.

When she sat down, Jake felt a little uneasy—not so much about what she had said, but how she had said it. There was a quiet peace about her as she talked. You could almost see the joy in her face as she talked about giving up this dream. Well, if Miss Betty could do that, maybe he and Lettie could give a few bucks.

There was special music, and then the pastor stood to speak. His topic, "Ground Zero—A Starting Point," suddenly came into focus. He was saying that God's work could be done if every member would simply wipe the slate clean and say, "Father, I have no preconceived opinions about what You want me to do. All that I ask is that You start with zero and show me what You want to do through me. I will, this morning, open my life to Your will as You seek to work it out through me."

The next day as Jake walked his route, he could not get that sermon off of his mind. Were there actually people who would open themselves to that kind of vulnerability about giving? Surely not. After he returned to the main office that afternoon, he shared his thoughts with Barney Bilby, another carrier. When he finished, Barney said, "Oh, I know what you mean. Our church had a program like that last year. I think I know what you are going through. Jake, I'll be praying for you in this."

That night at supper there was an odd quietness. Lettie didn't have much to say, and Jake found himself spending more time thinking than talking. Later in the evening, Lettie brought it up.

"Jake," she began, "I've been thinking about the service yesterday. Can you believe that testimony Miss Betty gave? I can't believe that woman would give up that trip. That's all she has talked about for as long as I can remember."

Lettie got out the material that had been mailed to them, and together they read about the need and about how the people were going to raise money to pay for it. The thing that surprised them was it seemed that the pastor and the people were serious about this "finding the will of God" stuff. As Jake said, "Frankly, I just wish someone would tell me what they want us to do. Then we could say a quick yes or no."

For whatever reason—I never got the whole story—Jake and Lettie were back in the service the next Sunday. The theme was the same, and it was reinforced with more testimonies and another powerful sermon. Always the emphasis was on finding His will rather than on giving money.

The following week was the most intense week ever in the marriage of Jake and Lettie. They talked about the church. They talked about what they had given to it. Jake remembered that the biggest thing he had ever done for the church was to provide the fish for the annual fish fry. He laughed when he said it, but Lettie detected an uneasiness in the laughter.

We will probably never know all that went on that week between Jake and Lettie, but on Saturday afternoon around 2:45, Jake called the pastor and met him for a cup of coffee down at the City Cafe. After a few minutes, the pastor asked Jake if he would share his story with the congregation the next morning. Jake had never talked before a group of people in his life, but for some reason, he agreed. The next morning, one very scared fisherman got up to speak.

He joked for a minute, and then he became very serious. "You folks know me and you know I'm not much on church. Lettie and me have spent more time worshipping at the lake than we have here with you.

"These past two weeks we have probably thought more about God and this church than we ever have in our lives. This morning I want to tell you what the result of all that thinking has been.

"Before I go on, I want Lettie to come up here and stand by me. She's in on this, too, and besides, I need her support."

He laughed an uneasy laugh as Lettie made her way to the platform. When she got there, she put her arm around him, and he started again.

"I guess me and Lettie have spent most of our lives fishing. A few years ago we decided to save up and buy a travel trailer. I'd planned to retire this year, and see, we'd go out and see America—mainly from the point of view of the lakeshores. A few months ago, I put in for retirement. We have the money in the bank for our trailer. We're ready to see that dream, our dream, come true.

"Well, we're changing our dream. As we looked at things, if we retire right now, we can't be a part of what this church, our church, is doing, and we want to be. Two years ago when Lettie was real sick, it was you people who took care of her. Sometime back when Pop died, it was you people and the preacher who were there.

"Well, now that the church needs something, we can't just ignore that. If I retire right now, we can't give anything because we will need it all to live on. So, last Friday, I went to my supervisor and withdrew my application for retirement. Now, don't get me wrong. Next month, I am going to buy that trailer, but it will just be three years older when we hit the road with it.

"By working for another three years, until I am sixty-five, we can give $10,000 to this building program. Somehow, right now, that just seems important to us."

Some people would describe Jake and Lettie as "good people who liked to fish." After hearing him that morning, I somehow feel that to say that about either of them would be to miss the point of who Jake and Lettie really were.

Perhaps it would be more appropriate to say that Jake and Lettie were just two people who dared to open themselves to the concept of "God through me."

▲ ▲ ▲
AN OBSERVATION
▼ ▼ ▼

I want to comment on the fact that, when it came time to share his testimony with the congregation, Jake told them how much he and Lettie were giving. Over the years, the giving of "specific dollar testimonies" has been one of the methods developed to help people in a congregation determine a level of sacrifice. Some churches and people are very comfortable using those type testimonies. In our company, when we design a program, we sometimes offer that as an option. Sometimes the people will choose that option, and at other times they may choose to communicate sacrifice in other ways.

But whether dollar amounts are given or not, there must be some way to example sacrifice for the people. In I Chronicles 29, when David was raising the money for the temple, he stood before the people and gave a specific dollar testimony. So there is a biblical precedent for the practice. But certainly, it is not for everyone.

Over the years, I have seen many people approach the time of sharing their personal decision about giving. Some will tell how much they are giving and some will not. But, in all my years in this ministry, I have seldom seen it be done boastfully. People who have prayed to seek God's will and then found that will for their lives typically come to the place David came to when he stood before the people and said,

> *"With all my resources I have provided for the temple of my God—gold for the gold work, silver for the silver, bronze for the bronze, iron for the iron and wood for the wood, as well as onyx for the settings, turquoise, stones of various colors, and all kinds of fine stone of various colors, and all kinds of fine stone and marble—all of these in large quantities.*
>
> *"Besides, in my devotion to the temple of my God I now give my personal treasures of gold and silver for the temple of my God, over and above everything I have provided for this holy temple...."*

I Chronicles 29:2 and 3 (NIV)

So David gave a testimony and his testimony was blessed by God when in verse 6 it is recorded,

> *"Then the leaders of families, the officers of the tribes of Israel, the commanders of thousands and commanders of hundreds,*

and the officials in charge of the king's work gave willingly. "

And later in verse 9,

"The people rejoiced at the willing response of their leaders, for they had given freely and wholeheartedly to the LORD. David the king also rejoiced greatly. "

My point is neither to condone nor condemn testimonies where a faithful saint of God shares the dollar amount of that testimony. It is to say that it can be done in such a way as to bring honor and glory to God. Would you not agree that David brought such honor and glory to God? Would you not agree that Jake and Lottie did exactly the same?

CHAPTER X

THE STANDARD

I am not certain how one would describe the church in suburban St. Paul, Minnesota, except to say that it was a "yuppie" church—the fellowship was comprised of a young, educated, upcoming generation. This in itself presented a unique opportunity to minister.

When our company first got involved with the church and made our initial studies, we were amazed at the demographics: average adult age, 34; average family income, $54,000; average number of children per family, 1.7; average years of education beyond high school, 3.1. As one elder commented, "The biggest problem we have in this church is how to get out of the parking lot without getting run over by a Mercedes."

It was with this kind of membership profile we entered into the development process for a major stewardship drive. It was because of this exact type situation that we, as a company, made the commitment years ago not to use the same program in every church. At RSI we have found every church to be unique. Certainly business as usual would not have been effective here.

Over a period of weeks, our staff in Dallas developed a game plan for the church in St. Paul. Hours on the phone, a few plane trips to discuss the program strategy with leadership, and we were ready to implement a plan for raising funds for the new building.

In any large church, the calendar is crucial. In St. Paul, it was especially so. The multitude of ministries coupled with the social outreach of the church meant that just getting time for the fund-raising drive would be difficult. Finally, we developed a four-month calendar with which both the church staff and our staff could work, and the project was launched.

From the beginning, it was a difficult program. Sometimes, no matter how well-developed the plan may be and how committed the church may be to the project, the program is simply not easy to lead. Often I am asked to review do-it-yourself approaches that fail, as so many of them do, and invariably it is because the organization hits difficult times and the church does not have leadership experienced in fund-raising skills to guide them through successfully.

Sometimes we, as a company, face the same situation, and it is only by drawing on the experience of our total staff that we are able to lead the church through to a successful completion. The program at St. Paul was like that. All the mechanical things were happening. The calendar dates were met. The organizations were staffing properly. If we needed twenty people in a meeting, we had twenty people. Promotional items were produced exactly on schedule.

The program was becoming an organizational success and a spiritual failure. There was no depth of sacrifice being shown. People were only casually approaching their personal commitment process. Spiritually, things were just not happening.

I remember sitting in my hotel room in St. Paul one evening after a meeting at the church. I was greatly concerned over what was taking place, or rather, what wasn't taking place.

We were three months into the program. On paper, it was a picture perfect program. Yet, it was not accomplishing what I had expected and wanted; i.e., spiritual renewal within the fellowship.

I remember trying to put my finger on the problem. The people were good people. The church leadership was excellent and totally committed to a spiritual experience through the stewardship effort. Our staff was committed to that type of experience. And yet, here we were, over halfway through the program and we were not accomplishing our primary objective.

In moments like this, I am reminded again that it is not from within us that the power for success comes, but only by the grace of God that our efforts bear fruit. That night as I reviewed every step, every meeting, every personality involved in the program, the light suddenly came on. The problem was not in the program. The problem was in the definition of sacrifice.

For three months, we had talked about sacrifice. But as I reviewed what was happening, it became clear to me that no standard of sacrifice had been set for the church to follow. We were talking conceptually, but there was no practical example for the people to follow.

Somewhere we had to find someone who would set the example of sacrifice and share the experience with the church. That night, I made the commitment to find that person.

Working with the pastor the next day, we identified three men who might be able to set the pattern of sacrifice through their personal commitment. Each man was a recognized leader in the church. Their spiritual commitment would not be in question.

Each of the three men was financially independent, so there was the possibility that the standard they set might represent a major contribution to the program itself. Each had indicated a willingness to provide leadership to the program.

With their names before us, the pastor picked up the phone and started setting appointments with our three prospective sacrificial pacesetters. To our surprise, all three were in town and appointments were set for us to see each of them individually. After a word of prayer together, we were on our way.

Our first visit was to Bob Jamison, a real estate developer who was one of the recognized "young turks" in the St. Paul area. We met at his office where he completely controlled the situation.   From our standpoint, his control was detrimental.

He took four phone calls during the thirty-minute meeting. His secretary interrupted us twice. Needless to say, we didn't accomplish what we wanted to accomplish. When we left, I had the distinct impression that this man should go into politics. He certainly had managed to avoid making a commitment on anything during our visit.

Our second visit was to George Davis.   The meeting was at his office, but George was the perfect host. His secretary was told to hold his calls, and for twenty minutes he gave us his complete attention. We explained how much a sacrificial gift could mean if it came from his family and how others would follow his leadership. After the need had been carefully explained, we paused for a reply.

George's eyes began to mist and slowly he started to speak, "Pastor, you can never know how I wish that I could do what is needed. But Pastor, Julie and I are getting a divorce. Because of that, you had better get someone else to fill this role."

With that word, his composure broke completely, and for the next few moments our mission was to carry a message of love and care—it was not to solicit funds.

After we got back into the car, the pastor said, "You know, you think you know your congregation, but I guess you never really know all that is going on in the lives of your people." We were learning how true this was as we continued to call on the people. Our next visit would prove equally interesting.

Doug and Barb O'Keefe had been one of the charter families at the St. Paul church. They had come to the city in the spring of 1975, the founding year for the church, and from their first day they had wanted to be a part of the "goin'est church" around.

They found their place in this small group, meeting in the pastor's home not three blocks from their own. Their first child had been killed in a school yard accident the year after they came to the church, and it had been the church people who had formed a circle of safety and caring around them.

Now, some nine years later, we were sitting in their lovely home, drinking coffee and talking about the stewardship program. There was a fire in the fireplace and their five-year-old daughter, Mary, sat in her mother's lap hugging her constant companion, a Cabbage Patch doll called "Suie."

"Susie" was just a little bit hard for this five-year-old to say.

During the course of the evening, Doug asked the pastor to give him a definition of sacrifice. The pastor simply said, "Doug, I don't know that I can define it for everyone, but to me, sacrifice is giving up something that is precious to me."

Looking around for an example, he said, "It would be like Mary giving up her 'Suie'." I noticed

Mary taking a very determined grip on the rather worn doll.

We left that night with Doug and Barb committed to giving serious thought and prayer to this business of sacrifice. Perhaps this committed couple would be the source of an example for everyone else to follow.

The pastor called me two days later to discuss the Sunday morning sermon. He was feeling a need to more clearly define sacrifice and wanted to discuss several approaches. We talked for several minutes, and finally he zeroed in on an approach that he would develop. Since I was to be in St. Paul on Sunday, he asked that I sit on the platform during the morning service and lead in a closing prayer of dedication and commitment.

Sunday came, and just by talking with him, I knew the pastor had prepared for this sermon perhaps as he had for no other in his ministry. There was an excitement about him as he discussed his approach.

"All week I have prayed about this sermon," he said. "I want this sermon to be simple enough that a child as young as Mary O'Keefe can understand it, and yet profound enough for the most educated here to be challenged by it."

"Pastor," I replied, "that will be a good one if you can pull it off."

With that doubtful word of encouragement, we walked to the platform.

Few times have I ever heard a man speak with more authority. His message of sacrifice was penetrating and disturbing. His audience reached out for every word as he developed his thesis. Simple? Perhaps so. Challenging? More so than I have ever heard before or since. The sermon was a masterpiece of biblical exposition. Surely if there was ever a message that would touch the lives of these wealthy, successful, educated people, this was it. Surely out of this hour we would find one of these businessmen who would come forward to say, "This is my sacrifice. Now let it be an example for others."

The pastor's closing appeal was even more touching. "God has laid before us a challenge at this time in the life of our church," he said. "This morning I am going to ask that if there is anyone here who is willing to sacrifice the most precious thing that you have in order for others of us to learn from you, I am going to ask that you come forward in a moment and tell me about your decision."

In that moment, even before the choir could begin a final hymn of decision, I saw what was about to happen. Slipping out from beside her father came little Mary O'Keefe. Before Doug could catch her, she had started up the aisle to where the pastor stood. Everyone on the platform and in the choir could see that she was holding "Suie" in her arms.

Without a word being said, this five-year-old child walked straight up to the pastor, and when he knelt down to receive her, she held out her hand and gave him "Suie." And then, without so much as a sound, she turned and walked back to her father.

Some who were there that morning later commented on how cute it was. Others made casual comments about the event. Practically everyone acknowledged that Mary had not really caught the deeper meaning of sacrifice.

But some of us who saw the immediate turnaround in the program knew that something significant had happened that morning. In a strange, unplanned, unprogrammed kind of way, the standard of sacrifice had been publicly set.

▲ ▲ ▲
An Observation
▼ ▼ ▼

One great lesson that must never be forgotten is this: never underestimate the power of children who come to know the joy of giving. Their examples can become staggering to the rest of us who seek His leadership in our lives.

At Southeast Christian Church in Louisville, Kentucky, there were several gifts in the $1 million range. But perhaps none were as influential as that of a young lad who gave the $130 he had been saving for over a year to buy his new bike.

In a program at First Baptist Church, Grapevine, Texas, the young people had been saving for a ski trip with the youth group. One Sunday a teenager shared her decision to give up the trip in order to support the building of a new educational building. When her father offered to send her anyway, she answered, "No, Dad. I want to look back someday and know that at least once in my life I set the right priorities."

The three children of a family in Detroit went to the dinner table one evening and asked their parents if they would disconnect cable TV and pledge that $35 per month to the church building program. Later the father confessed to me that after the first few months they saw a dramatic change in the family. They talked more and the children read more, school grades went up. These were just a few of the by-products of children who took seriously the search for sacrifice.

Don't ever underestimate the power of children when it comes to discovering the joy of giving. They will often set a very high standard for those of us who think we are more "mature" in our Christian walk.

CHAPTER XI

ONE MOMENT

I t is curious how a single moment in time, separated from the millions of moments allowed in life, can dramatically change the direction of one's life. That fact is evidenced in the lives of most of us.

I once talked with Rubin Bergman who has dedicated himself to a lifetime of law with a specialty in war crime prosecution. As a child of seven, he had seen his mother and sister taken to the gas chambers in Auschwitz. He described that moment of separation as a split second in time when he dedicated himself to getting out and getting even. That moment changed his life.

The same was true for Olympic Gold Medalist Kathy Rigsby. Told by a gym teacher at age eight that she should give up gymnastics, she decided in that moment to become the best in the world. Seven years later with the world watching, she proved that the commitment made in a moment of anger and determination was a valid one.

This story is about a single moment in a young boy's life. A defining moment that seemed so insignificant to others that it was soon forgotten. But a moment so important to him that it would change the direction of his life for more than thirty years. This is the story of Chuck Rogers.

Basketball is big in Indiana. That may be the understatement of the ages. From the moment a boy child in Indiana is born, his height measurement is followed to see if he will be a potential Indiana University star. In Indiana, you have to be over six feet tall just to be a trainer!

From grade school in Blackhawk, Indiana, a suburb of Ft. Wayne, it was evident that Chuck Rogers was one of the chosen few. He was the only boy in the fourth grade who was as tall as the girls in his class. This kid was going to be big. Couple that with a natural ability to handle the ball, and you have the making of success.

Coach Billings, the basketball coach at Blackhawk Elementary, recognized ability and talent. Chuck had both, and he soon became the coach's prime student. Practice after-hours, skull sessions, anything necessary to turn him into a great player was given to this kid who could one day be IU material. Who knows, maybe even the NBA would not be out of the question.

The coach and the student had a bond that was tangible. Fortunately, Coach Billings was the kind of influence to which you would want to expose a young boy in grammar school.

The fourth and fifth grades were completed. A good student and an athlete all in one body was fast moving into the competitive lanes.

Parallel to the developing basketball story in Chuck's life was an equally influential home life. In a nutshell, the Roger's home life was about to explode. Chuck's father, for years the idol of the young man, was about to take every step possible to destroy the image that his son held of him.

In September, one week after school opened, his father came home and beat up his mother in front of Chuck and his two sisters. Later in September, his father attacked Kathy, Chuck's younger sister; a beating so bad the child was hospitalized for ten days.

After these episodes, Chuck's mother sat him down and shared for the first time the facts about her life with his father—a life of abuse, both physically and mentally. How, wondered Chuck, was it possible to live in the same house with his parents and not know this was going on? He had no answer to the question, but the growing openness of his father's abusive ways washed from his mind any possible doubt.

On October 3rd of his sixth year in school, his mother called the three children together and announced that she could take it no longer. She was filing for divorce. She was getting out and taking her children with her.

For the next year, Chuck lived in a hell of torn emotions. He loved his mother, but he also loved his father. This was the man who took him fishing and shot baskets with him. This was the man who called almost every night, who still came by to visit, and who took him on those private outings that mean so much to a son.

But this was also the man who called Christmas Eve to say that he would be over in about an hour and never showed. This was the man who wrote a letter to Chuck six months later to say that he was living in California and hoped to see him again soon. Chuck didn't hear from him again for over thirty years.

All of that in the sixth grade. No wonder Chuck's grades fell. No wonder his interest in sports passed. No wonder life seemed so useless and wasted.

Chuck's mother made the change from housewife and mother to breadwinner and mother, and immediately their lifestyle changed. Chuck's father had been a good provider, but when he walked out he walked out completely. The house payment was still due the month after he left. The car payment was due. The country club dues came around and three children still needed food.

Within three months, the family went from a home with a mortgage in Blackhawk Heights to an apartment in the low-rent district on Pall Street. If you wanted to know about transition from wealth to poverty, all you had to do was study the Rogers family. Theirs was a textbook case.

One thing that happens in such a change is the development of new friendships at different socioeconomic levels. Whereas in the past Chuck's friends spent Saturday afternoon at the club playing tennis, his new friends on Pall Street were more likely to hang out down at the public park. Not necessarily bad, but different.

Making ends meet became a family affair. His older sister Ann took an afternoon job at the drug store. His younger sister Kathy had the responsibility of keeping house while his mother worked two jobs. Chuck got a job at the local Chevrolet dealer cleaning the shop area. It was a team effort, and they were making it work. Although there was also an empty spot where a father had once been, there was still a roof over their heads and food on the table, and there was a generous amount of love.

For the next three years, the pattern of life was rather routine: work, school, home. Bills were paid, but there was not one extra dime for luxury. In fact, it would have been a disaster if anyone in the family had needed a doctor. Each Saturday when the family came together, they would pool their week's earnings, pay the bills, and marvel that no matter how they tried, nothing was ever left over.

During this time, there was little room for basketball. A Saturday afternoon game at the YMCA, a parking lot pick-up game on Saturday, or an occasional game at school was about the extent of Chuck's athletic career. He was still talented and tall and he loved the game. He just didn't have time for it.

Basketball team tryouts were announced on the first day of his sophomore year in high school. To play high school basketball in Ft. Wayne was the first step for many a young man seeking fame and fortune on the courts. Following the encouragement of his friends, Chuck showed up for tryouts. The way he walked, the confidence he exuded, and the physical conditioning he maintained signaled to the coaches that this kid was a natural.

His performance matched their expectations: eight out of ten free throws; six out of ten hooks made while being guarded by the previous year's star guard; wind sprints that barely left him winded. This kid was all-star material if ever there was.

When the roster was posted the next day, Chuck Rogers read his name on the list. But the thrill left almost immediately. Right by his name was the time for practice the next day—3:45 p.m. in the high school gymnasium. Chuck knew he had a problem. In the excitement of tryouts, he had failed to take into consideration his work schedule. The time conflict between practice and his job was unavoidable.

There were no options for Chuck. He did not work by choice, but rather out of necessity. He informed the coaches that he could not make the practices, and therefore, he was released from the team. At least he did not have to turn in his uniform. They were to be passed out the next day at practice.

For the next few days, Chuck bordered on a classic case of teenage depression. It would have been easy to drop out and hate the world then. Why was life unfair? Why did he have to work when other kids played? Where was his old man when he really needed him? But resentment was not a trait inherited from his mother. If she was made of stronger stuff, then so was he. In a couple of weeks he pulled out of it and life returned to its basic patterns: school, work, home, and school again—and, oh yes, don't forget the Saturday afternoon pick-up games down at the park.

One Saturday, six of the guys were playing a rough and rugged game when Coach Billings walked up. Chuck had not seen his old grammar school coach in a while and it was good to talk to him again. In the course of the conversation, Chuck explained his home situation and told the coach of his short, one-day basketball career.

In return, Chuck found that Coach Billings was no longer coaching in the school system. He had taken a job with a manufacturing company in town, and his coaching was limited to the local Boys Club team. A team that played a full inner-city schedule and practiced four nights a week at the clubhouse.

The minute the practice schedule was mentioned, Chuck saw his opportunity. What would be the possibility of his being on the Boys Club team?

With a smile, Billings replied, "The possibility is pretty good. You don't think I spend my Saturday afternoons at city parks watching pick-up games for nothing, do you? The next practice is Monday night at 7:30. I'll expect you there."

From the moment Chuck joined the Hilldale Boys Club team, not another team in town had a prayer.

Who would have believed that a sophomore kid, the youngest boy on the team, could have made such a difference. The first game of the season was with Riverside; the final score: Hilldale-87, Riverside-53. Chuck had scored 28 points.

As the season progressed, Hilldale got better and Chuck consistently led the team in scoring. The scores in Hilldale's favor were almost embarrassing: Hilldale-66, Southside-22; Hilldale-81, Longview-77; Hilldale-95, Conner-36. Local newspapers had picked up on the story so often that the high school coaches in the area began to complain that the Hilldale's Boys Club team was getting more coverage than the local high school teams.

Chuck was also gaining a following as the kid who was making it happen in basketball in Ft. Wayne. For years, the Boys Club teams were lucky to draw 50 fans, and those fans were usually parents and a few friends who came to watch the kids play. With Chuck on the team, the Hilldale team began to draw crowds. Not just a few, but hundreds!

Back then in Indiana, the Boys Club had a full state structure with city-wide play-offs that ultimately ended with a state championship. Obviously, Hilldale would go to state from Ft. Wayne since no other team in the city could match their talent. It would be interesting to see what happened at the state play-offs in Indianapolis. It took only one long weekend of play-offs to realize that Hilldale was no freak team. These kids were good and Chuck Rogers was unbelievable.

On Friday night of the play-off weekend, Hilldale beat a team from Lexington by a score of 87-58. Lexington had been unbeaten. On Saturday afternoon they beat the number one team from Huntsville by a score of 78-77. Huntsville had been unbeaten. On Sunday afternoon, they would play the number one team from Indianapolis, the Westside Bullets, for the championship. Westside was made up of boys who had played together for three years, and for three years they had won the championship. The Bullets were good and they knew it. They were ready for Hilldale.

The game had received excessive press coverage in the Indianapolis papers. Feature stories were written on the boys and their backgrounds. College scouts attended the game and were interviewed. Reporters wrote the story of Chuck Rogers and how he was playing for the Hilldale team because he had to work and could not practice with his high school team. It was a good story in itself, but by the time the reporters got through with it, it was the kind of stuff of which movies are made.

More than 8,000 spectators packed the Civic Center for Sunday afternoon's play-off game. No game, Boys Club or high school, had ever drawn that kind of attendance in Indianapolis, and these people did not come to cheer a team. The people were coming to see Chuck Rogers, the 6'8" first-year kid from Ft. Wayne. Seven thousand, nine hundred and eighty-nine ordinary people, plus twelve college recruiting scouts had paid their money to see the kid play.

From the opening tip-off, Chuck did not disappoint them. Everything he did was right. If his guard went up with him, he hooked off and scored. If the inside was tight, he shot what in pro basketball would now be a three-pointer. And when he shot, he scored. By half-time, Chuck had personally scored 24 points. Hilldale was under his leadership and they were beating the former champions by a half-time score of 36-33. It was a great game!

At the risk of being insensitive, I must explain a situation that fortunately had not been reported in the papers. It concerns Chuck and his preparation for the game. Shirts and shorts were the only parts of the uniform provided by the Boys Club—no socks, no shoes, no underwear. Chuck had improvised an athletic supporter by putting on a pair of boxer shorts and tying the legs up with shoe strings on each side. Why? He simply couldn't afford an athletic supporter, so he had done what he had become accustomed to doing ever since his father left home. He made do.

With the half-time pep talks over, the game resumed. If Chuck was hot the first half, he was blazing the second half. His first eight shots were good. At seven minutes into the third period, he had a string of nine consecutive free throws. The crowd loved it. They cheered, they chanted his name, they stomped the bleachers with every shot. Even though he tried not to pay attention, Chuck knew this was his game and he revelled in it. With three minutes to play in the third period, Hilldale led by 18 points. They were on their way to winning the championship.

There's always that moment that can change a person's life for years and years to come. With two minutes and thirty-two seconds on the clock in the third period of the championship game in the Civic Center in Indianapolis, Indiana, that moment came for Chuck Rogers. For in that moment, he stood at the free throw line to shoot a foul shot and he heard the gentle ripple of laughter begin to replace the cheers. Not understanding their laughter, he looked to the crowd for an explanation. Suddenly, he understood. It was at that moment he realized that the string holding his boxer shorts up had broken, and slipping out from under the leg of his blue uniform for eight thousand people to see were his white with red polka dot undershorts. With tears of embarrassment, Chuck looked into the faces of the thousands as they roared with laughter at his expense.

In total humiliation, Chuck dropped the basketball and walked to the dressing room. And with every step he said, "I will never be poor again. I will never be poor again. I will never be poor again."

In the dressing room, he dressed quickly, walked outside, and hitchhiked home to Ft. Wayne. That moment in time molded his life for the next thirty years. He never picked up a basketball again.

To succeed in other fields became an obsession. Chuck withdrew into himself for the next two years of high school and he studied hard, obsessed with getting into college. He earned a scholarship to the Texas A & M engineering school, where he completed his four-year course study in three years.

He took a graduate degree in engineering, always working hard to be the best in the class. He worked night and weekend jobs to help pay expenses. He was going to succeed, he was going to succeed big, and he was going to do it in Indianapolis.

After completing his master's degree, he was offered a position in a firm in Houston at a starting salary of $12,500 per year. He turned it down to take a lesser paying job in Indianapolis. To make it in Indianapolis was an obsession.

By his second year in Indianapolis, he had positioned himself in the firm and had married the daughter of a prominent family. His obsession was tempered a bit by the fact that "things" didn't seem to have such an important place in Ann's life. Of course, she had "things" all of her life. Also, she had not been the one standing at the free throw line with eight thousand people laughing. To this day, Chuck could bring the emotions and the determination to the surface by just repeating, "I will never be poor again! I will never be poor again!"

One project followed another until at age thirty-four, he was made a full partner in the firm. He now had money, he had position, he had family, and he had the constant fear that it all could end at any moment. If he had a bedtime prayer it might have gone something like this, "Now I lay me down to sleep. I pray the Lord my wealth to keep. Dear God, don't let me ever be poor again."

By this time, he and Ann had become quite active in a local Methodist church. It was as if Chuck had found his niche in life. He had a lovely wife, two beautiful children, a comfortable home, a growing professional following, and a deepening religious commitment. But he also had the haunting fear that it could end. It is said that some people have the monkey of drugs on their back. Chuck's monkey was just as real. And every night in the darkness it was with him—"I will never be poor again."

Yet, over all those years after he returned to Indianapolis, no one associated Charles Rogers of White, Williams, and Rogers Engineering Firm with the kid who got laughed out of the Civic Center. That event had long been forgotten by everyone except Chuck. For years, he had visualized and fantasized about someday getting everyone back. If he had just been able to get the proper setting, he would have said for all to hear, "Look here, people. I'm the one who was laughed off the basketball court. You laughed, but look at me now. I've made it, turkeys! I've made it!"

But that time never came. The years passed, and after a while it just didn't seem as important to get everyone back. The important thing was to keep making money so that poverty would not become a reality again. It was now an imbedded personal battle that Chuck fought. And it struggled within his being for almost forty years!

I was there the night the change in Chuck's life was publicly announced. It came at an Advance Commitment Dinner in the middle of a stewardship program at the Methodist church where Chuck and Ann were members.

Earlier in the month, the pastor had asked Chuck to give his personal testimony to the people attending this particular dinner. He had asked Chuck to relate the process that he and Ann had gone through in making their decision, and if possible, to tell how much they were going to give.

Two days before the dinner, Chuck called me in Dallas and asked if it would be possible to meet at his office on the afternoon of the dinner. He wanted to talk about his testimony. That afternoon I flew into Indianapolis, grabbed a bite to eat, and went to see him. Having done this a thousand times, I did not expect anything unusual or different.

After the usual social greeting, Chuck told me what he had in mind for the evening. As he laid out the outline of the testimony, he said, "Ben, I have some standing in this community. Last year I was chairman of the Indianapolis Mayor's Commission, and following that I was urged to run for the U.S. Senate. The public is still expecting me to run for something, be it mayor, governor, or dogcatcher. What would you think if I asked the press to be present for my speech at the dinner tonight? Do you think my testimony, given the unique background of it, could touch the lives of others out there if they read it in the papers or hear about it on TV?"

Usually, I would have immediately said this was a terrible idea. With the decision being so very personal, it is often unwise to bring outside influences into the dinners. But in view of the relationship of this man and the people of this city, I gave the okay. He pressed the proper buttons, and that evening we met in one of the most beautiful homes in Indianapolis with forty guests and press coverage that included both newspapers and the local ABC TV affiliate.

After the meal, the pastor introduced me and I said a few words. Then Charles Rogers was introduced. As he stood to speak, the TV lights were turned on, microphones were raised, and everyone there waited to hear what this was all about. Certainly, I had never been to an Advance Commitment Dinner like this and I felt certain no one else had either.

Chuck played it like a pro. He displayed professional posters made with the headlines from the sports page of February 11, 1955. It read "Westside Overcomes Hilldale 88-79!" Standing before the people and before the cameras, he unfolded the story. No detail was spared. He told of his father leaving and what it had done to his family. He told of his mother's determination to hold the family together. He spoke of afternoon jobs and late night discussions about money.

But most of all, he told of an experience in the Civic Center in Indianapolis and a moment that literally set the course of his life. A few of the old guards reached deep into their memories and were able to recall the event. Most had to take Chuck's word for it. But all of them listened because they were intrigued with his story.

As he began to close, he came specifically to the point at which he walked off the court and the forming of a lifetime slogan that, simply stated, had molded his life. Those six simple words: "I will never be poor again."

By this time, tears flowed down his face. Charles Rogers is a big man, a rugged man who rides horses and drives fast cars, but at this moment, he opened the window of his soul for an entire town to see. Finally, he came to the close.

"From the moment I walked out of the Civic Center that day and hitchhiked back to Ft. Wayne, I have dedicated my life to getting what is mine. If there are three words that have been the focus of my life, they have been 'my, my, my.' Every moment of every day for thirty years I have had that inward selfish focus. I am here tonight to inform you that from that standpoint, it has been a life of hell. My experience tells me that you can never get enough to satisfy that need.

"Two months ago, I got involved in this program to raise money for the new sanctuary. From the beginning, we were told that the only thing we would be asked to do would be to take seriously the search for God's will in this matter. Ann and I took that as a serious and worthy challenge.

"Two weeks ago I made a life-changing discovery. I discovered that all of these things that I have spent my life gathering are not mine at all. No matter how I have tried, I have never owned them. In reality, they have owned me. Two weeks ago after making that discovery, Ann and I got on our knees in our living room and committed everything back to Him. With that, our prayers became 'Lord, what do You want to do through us for Your glory?'

"Tonight I stand before you to tell you that for the first time in all of these years, I feel free. We have nothing to give. We really own nothing. But of what God has entrusted to our keeping we are giving a gift of $450,000 to this program. That amount represents our total liquid assets. We have nothing else but the assurance of God that we—no, I—will never be poor again."

The news media reported the evening. Not in headlines, but they did give it coverage. Across the city the following morning, people read the story and then hurried off to work. The newspapers had carried the story as a story of poverty. The radio-TV media considered it a story of wealth. At the Roger's home, it was seen as a story of freedom.

▲ ▲ ▲
AN OBSERVATION
▼ ▼ ▼

So many people around us are chained to their commitment to things. A few years ago, I was in California riding down the freeway with a friend of mine. For several months, I had seen him struggle with some battle unknown to me.

As we talked that afternoon he talked to me about his financial situation. He shared his concern and insecurity about the future. Finally, he commented, "I just need some reserves. I am putting every extra dollar I make into savings. If I can ever get a $100,000 in savings, I think I will feel secure."

What he didn't know or understand is that he can never save enough to feel secure. Security is usually not a financial matter. Security is an image matter. Security is the peace that comes by resting in the hands of God, not resting in the knowledge of savings.

Now that is not to say that we are not to be wise stewards of the possessions God entrusts to us. But that must not be where the security lies.

A few years later, I saw my friend again. He had his $100,000 and much more in savings. But he was still insecure. He was still frightened. He was the mirror image of the old Charles Rogers.

If I could pray for one blessing to be known by all of us, it would be freedom. Whether we have meager possessions or millions my prayer would be the same—"Lord, give us the joy of being free from all those things that own us."

CHAPTER XII

ALL ACCOUNTS PAID IN FULL

I n a hospital room with his wife of sixty-three years
by his side, Uncle Louie Schultz died. The day he
died, all of his accounts were marked "Paid In Full."

This is one of only two stories in this selection
where the people are real and their names and locations
have not been changed. It has been many years since
I first met Uncle Louie and Aunt Mamie. Even now as
I think back through this experience from my early
ministry, I must admit that some of the facts may even
be wrong.

But the important thing is that you come to know
these people as I did, and that all of us learn from their
"life lessons" of giving.

Uncle Louie and Aunt Mamie Schultz were real
people and they probably taught me more about giving
and the giving spirit than all the others put together.

In 1965, I went to First Baptist Church in La
Grange, Texas, as the new pastor. I was fresh out of
seminary and after a series of college and seminary
part-time churches, I finally had my first full-time
parish. It was a place to make mistakes and to learn,
to fail one day and to succeed the next. It was a place

where people loved you in spite of your inexperience. It was a place where people allowed you to love them in return. It was the ideal first pastorate.

My first week on the church field, I heard about Uncle Louie and Aunt Mamie. At that time they were in their eighties, had been married well over fifty years, were charter members of First Baptist Church, and were the adopted aunt and uncle of everyone in town. It seemed to me that this would be the perfect place to start my pastoral visitation.

I called to set up the appointment and we mutually agreed that 3:00 the next afternoon would be perfect. I later learned that Aunt Mamie insisted on having that much time before the visit in order to make Uncle Louie "whack" the carpets and "swish" the blinds before the new preacher arrived.

You cannot imagine my surprise when Uncle Louie answered the door. By this time, I had heard so many stories about this man that I must have expected a giant. To my surprise there stood a little old man about five feet tall, bent over with arthritis, waiting to greet me.

With a firm handshake, he pulled me into the living room and introduced me to Aunt Mamie. Aunt Mamie was about four feet ten inches in high heels, weighed about 80 pounds, and on this day, was dressed in her finest. From that moment on, the hour was hers.

First of all she pointed me to a chair with a stern, "Not that one, young man, that's Louie's chair."

Then she served coffee and cookies on the daintiest of silk napkins. From that first hour, she had me. I do not mean to imply that she had me only as a friend. She had me wrapped around her finger completely. She talked about her life as a Christian and her life as a Baptist and her life in La Grange and her life with Louie. Occasionally, she would punctuate it all with, "Now isn't that the way it was, Louie?"

And what a story it was. Uncle Louie had immigrated to the United States as a young man. As so many of the German people now living in South Texas, he had come to America with little more than the clothes on his back.

He had started work for the railroad when he was very young. On the wall in the living room the day of my first visit was a plaque that attested to his fifty years of faithful service. He had fallen in love with Mamie and courted her, and almost as children, they had been married.

What a beautiful story it would be to say that their life together was all love and music. But that was not so. Their marriage was childless even though they often prayed that God would send them a baby. Their home burned. Often illness swept the country, and they suffered with others who were stricken.

Uncle Louie would often be gone for days on end with his job on the railroad. During those times, Aunt Mamie was the one who "defended the fort," as she said, and made the home a safe haven for Louie's return.

They told me of their involvement in the start-up of First Baptist Church. They talked about how some did not want to build a building, but how Uncle Louie had made a "fire-spittin'" speech that just got the thing moving.

Uncle Louie told about working on the roof of the tall second-story building, and being so afraid of falling that he would come down and be physically ill from the tension. But as he said, "Preacher, if I hadn't led the way and started putting the roof on back there in 1920, you would probably get rain on your head the next time it rains."

That was the philosophy of Uncle Louie and Aunt Mamie. If it needs to be done, then do it. If you pray for a roof, then take up the hammer that God gives you and put one on. A few hours with Aunt Mamie and Uncle Louie and one really understood how the West was won.

When I had been called to the pastorate of First Baptist Church, one of the things that was obvious was the need to relocate. The church had been considering relocation for years, but for a number of reasons it had just never gotten off the ground.

I am sure no one would admit it, but I imagine that one of the concerns was how Uncle Louie and Aunt Mamie would feel about it. After all, their life was symbolic of the sacrifice that was needed to build the present structure. But the fact remained that the building was old and a new structure would soon become a necessity.

Being a good Baptist church, we spent months in preparation studies before the recommendation was given. About a month before we were to present the recommendation to the congregation for a vote to sell the old building and start the relocation process, I made a call on Uncle Louie and Aunt Mamie.

I remember how tentative I was as I explained that the recommendation would be made in the next business meeting to sell the present church and purchase land out on the edge of town to build another new church building.

After my initial statements, we started to talk about the church and what God was doing with us. We talked about those early days and laughed about the time Aunt Mamie picked up a hammer and started to nail nails in the wall. As she later said, "I just wanted those workmen to know that thirty minutes was long enough for anyone to take for lunch. It was time to get back to work!"

We talked about the weddings and funerals they had witnessed in that building. We rejoiced over people who had been brought into the kingdom as a result of the preaching there.

Aunt Mamie brought out her book and went down a list of pastors who had served there. I remember well that as she got to one pastor (who shall remain nameless) she said, "Preacher, that man was just worthless. Just lazy, that's all he was." And then with a twinkle in her eye, she said, "And if you don't eat another one of my cookies, that's what I am going to tell everyone else about you, too."

After we had shared all of the stories again and the book had been put away, Uncle Louie looked me straight in the eye and said, "Well, if it needs to be done, let's do it."

Often I work with churches that are trying to relocate and I see people who try to block the progress. They are often well-intentioned people, but people who have come to believe that the church is a building. When I see or hear from those kind of people, I remember Uncle Louie and his, "Well, if it needs to be done, let's do it."

A few weeks later, we went to the congregation and voted yes to the proposal. We would immediately begin a fund-raising program to raise the money.

Now you have to understand that First Baptist Church, La Grange, Texas, had never had a fund-raising program of any kind. In fact, the morning that we voted to enter into this one, the chairman of the deacons pulled me aside just before the vote and said, "Preacher, just for your information, the last preacher that preached on stewardship around here was asked to leave. You sure you want to go through with this?"

All pastors should have such supportive deacons!

In spite of that, the church voted unanimously to move forward. After the service, Uncle Louie asked me to stop by their house that afternoon. When I got there, I was presented with the first pledge on the new building.

It was written on the back of a simple piece of white paper torn from a child's school tablet. The commitment was not large for their resources were meager, but it set the pace for what was about to happen in the church.

Over the next year, we sold the downtown property and purchased new property for the new church site. We completed the first capital stewardship program in the church's history. We started construction on the new church facility, and we watched day by day as it moved toward completion.

The sacrifice of Aunt Mamie and Uncle Louie that set the pace for the rest of us was not in vain. We actually did complete the project that we started out to complete.

But that is not what this story is all about. This story is about Aunt Mamie and Uncle Louie, so let me tell you how it ends.

All the people had made three-year pledges on the building. They gave, and with their gifts and with a loan made to the church, we were able to begin and complete construction. By doing this, we were able to be in our new building even before the three-year period ran out.

We had been in the new building about two months when I received a call from the hospital that I was needed by Aunt Mamie. Uncle Louie had slipped into a coma and was not expected to live through the night.

For four days, we sat around the clock with this dear tiny old man as his life slipped away. At times, he would stir a bit, but for the most part, it was a quiet and restful approach to death. Elizabeth Wylie, a dear friend of mine, and the closest thing to a daughter that Aunt Mamie and Uncle Louie had, sat there, too, waiting for the end to come.

It was about three o'clock on a Wednesday afternoon that we heard Uncle Louie trying to get out of bed. Quickly, we rushed to his bedside only to realize that from somewhere within his coma, he was attempting to speak.

We leaned over to hear the whisper as he said, "Mamie, get me a check." Touching his forehead with her old wrinkled hand as she must have done a thousand times through the years, she whispered back, "It's okay, Louie. I'm here with you. Go back to sleep now."

But Uncle Louie was not to be outdone. This time he raised up from the pillow, and with as much strength as he could muster said, "Mamie, I said get me a check."

Aunt Mamie looked at me and with hurt and bewilderment said, "Pastor, I don't know what he wants. I don't have a check. What should I do?"

Quickly looking around the room, I saw a newspaper. I picked it up and tore a section out about the size of a check. Then I placed it in the hand of Uncle Louie and said, "It's okay, Uncle Louie, here is a check for you."

Then, again using what seemed to be his last bit of strength, he asked for a pen. I took a pen out of my pocket and gave it to him. And then this dying man took the pen and made a few illegible marks on the paper and gave it back to me.

With a deep sigh of relief and exhaustion, he lay back in bed. After just a moment or two, we heard his whisper, "I just couldn't meet God behind on my pledge." And then he died.

A few days after the funeral, I took the opportunity to look the pledge records up. At that time, we were twenty-eight months into a thirty-six month pledge period. Never once had Uncle Louie and Aunt Mamie been behind on their pledge. At the time of his death, the only "back payment" was for the previous week.

Uncle Louie had missed that payment, the payment that caused his concern, because he had been in the hospital, in a coma, dying.

Sometime later, Aunt Mamie died. Their full estate, including their home and surrounding land, was left to First Baptist Church.

▲ ▲ ▲
AN OBSERVATION
▼ ▼ ▼

For the church of tomorrow, we are, to a great extent, facing a generation of people who don't know how to give. It is not ingrained into their being. Where are the Uncle Louie stories going to come from in the future?

A couple of years ago we did a study to determine where people learned to give. The respondents fell into three very distinct age categories. They were:

GROUP ONE—AGE 55 AND OLDER
    This group almost always learned to give at home. They told stories of fathers who set the example or mothers who were faithful in teaching them to give. We heard comments like the man who said, "Every week I received a fifty-cent allowance and in the name of the Lord my Mom ripped off the first dime." Giving was taught in the home.

GROUP TWO—AGES 35 TO 55
    Here we found a mixture of stewardship mentors. Some talked of home and others mentioned church. Sunday School teachers, preachers, family members were all given as examples. But almost across the board this group could identify those who influenced them.

GROUP THREE—AGES 20 TO 35
With few exceptions, this group absolutely amazed and astounded us. Within this group there was no clear understanding or personal definition of giving. In fact, at one point in the study we asked the respondents to define their most vivid giving experience and over 50 percent of them defined an experience where they *received* something!

There seemed to be an attitude of buying services rather than giving gifts. Some in this group talked about their giving to the church much like their buying a ticket to the movie. "When I go to the movie on Saturday, I pay $6 for a ticket and I see a movie. When I go to church on Sunday, I give $6 and I participate in the services."

"But," we asked, "what happens when you don't go to church the next Sunday?"

Without hesitation they replied, "The same thing that happens if I don't go to the movie. I didn't get anything, so I didn't buy a ticket. I didn't go to church, so I didn't get anything. So why would I give?"

There are nights when I lie awake trying to find a solution to this generational wave now moving through the church—a wave of people who don't understand the whole concept of Christian giving. Twenty years from now these people will be the leaders of the church. These will be the people setting the standard for their generation.

So I ask you once again: where are the Uncle Louie stories going to come from in the days and years ahead? I am haunted by the lack of an adequate answer.

CHAPTER XIII

IT'S NOT HARD TO GIVE

As the sun began to set across the Southern California sky, Jerry Williamson settled back on a worn-out couch and surveyed the three rooms he planned to call home. The old wooden house was dark and smelled of the heat even with the windows open, but enough light streamed through the trees in the yard to fill the rooms with shadows. Jerry could see most of the house from where he sat.

The small living room sat between a small bedroom and an even smaller kitchen where flowered tiles had begun to fade on the wall above the stove. Wallpaper in the living room consisted of Sunday's comics from two years earlier that had yellowed and cracked and peeled until it covered only spots in the center of each wall. He looked around the house and thought to himself, "Well, Jerry. For a guy who is broke, black and crippled, I guess you are doing pretty good."

Jerry reached down and lifted his heavily braced legs onto the couch. If planned correctly, he thought, unpacking could be a project that would keep him busy for days. Pots and pans and clothes lay strewn in boxes on the living room floor. Windows needed washing, and the wood floors needed repairs. Jerry welcomed the mess, as he was not sure what would keep him busy when he finished. He knew no one in this city, just as he had known no one in his hometown. He had lived off disability checks for the past three years and had found little reason to leave the house.

He had nothing in particular to look forward to here. The move to Wimberly had been merely an escape from a painful past. He did not expect, nor wish, that his life here would be any different than it had been in his hometown. At nineteen years old, Jerry settled down for life as a friendless, lonely old man.

From his vantage point on the couch, Jerry could look out the window into a bright neighborhood of old homes and short, stubby trees. The houses were small and identical, but yards were well-kept and neatly fenced.

The church stood less than a quarter of a mile down the road. It was a gigantic building that covered most of the block. Its steeple pointed twice as high as any other building in the area, and a sign with bold black letters sat on the lawn. Jerry gazed out the window at a slow moving mass of people that had begun to file out the church doors. He watched with mild curiosity as the crowd trickled off into smaller groups that laughed and talked as they walked towards their cars filling the parking lot and lining the streets.

There was a time when the sight of people laughing together would have made him feel depressed, but years of disappointments had hardened him. He had quit school in the second grade to escape the teasing about his braces and crutches. He spent the days in his room at home, remembering the humiliation and the tears. He hated people for forcing his seclusion, and he hated God for allowing it to happen. He blocked out the world for fear they would laugh, until one day, he found himself as a grown man, alone. He learned to forgive, then to forget, and then he gave up. Although he had not found friends, Jerry rarely thought much about being lonely anymore.

The groups from the church were slowly scattering off in different directions. Those who walked down Johnson Street passed so close to Jerry's house that he could have talked to them through his window without leaving the couch. Of course, that would have been unthinkable. Even if he normally spoke to strangers, Jerry never would have approached this group. These people were educated, well-dressed, and white. If he had met them on the street, he would have crossed out of their way. Until the group passed, Jerry felt out of place, even in his own home.

As the evening sky turned from orange to gray, Jerry eyed the last few stragglers at the church door. He watched with amusement as a man sat on the steps and listened intently to the words of a small boy. The man was huge, and the boy looked like an insignificant bystander in the scene. But when the conversation was finished, the two shook hands with the seriousness of equals.

The man waved a goodbye to the remaining people on the steps and turned toward Johnson Street.

It took only minutes for him to make his way to Jerry's house.

Jerry watched the man's progress and realized that there must be some mistake. He was probably looking for the former resident, Jerry decided, and he positioned his crutches to raise himself from the couch. He barely had time to stand when he saw the man waiting patiently on the other side of the screen door. Jerry moved to the door and waited for him to ask for someone else.

"Good evening, Mr. Williamson," the man said. "My name is Don Bates. A friend of mine said you just moved in."

The man paused, but Jerry said nothing. If he knows who I am, he thought, why is he here?

"I teach a Bible class at Zion Community Church across the street. I just wanted to drop by and invite you to join us next Sunday."

Jerry was confused. Here was a white man dressed in a suit and tie, standing at the door of a black man's house, asking him to come to church.

Bates was waiting calmly on the porch for a reply. Jerry asked him inside only because he had no idea what else to do.

Bates sat on the couch with Jerry and talked about the city, his friends in the church, the weather. This was a good place to live, he said, and he hoped Jerry would enjoy being part of the community. Jerry politely answered the man's questions about his home and his family, and he listened quietly as Bates spoke.

"We can give you a ride to the church if the walk's too much for you. Wouldn't want a little thing like that to keep you away."

Jerry smiled and thanked the man for his offer.

"Well, we'd certainly be glad to have you," and he stood to leave. The two men shook hands at the door, and the man made his way out the gate and down Johnson Street.

As the dusk turned to darkness, Jerry followed the man's movements under the street lights as he made his way back towards the church. He laughed quietly to himself at the thought of picking up his crutches to join a bunch of educated, rich people at church.

"You're welcome any time," Mr. Bates had said, "even if you just want to meet some new friends."

Jerry's smile faded, and his expression grew serious. How long had it been since someone had talked with him as long as this stranger had? He could not remember anyone ever being interested in his life. In his hometown, Jerry had shut out neighbors and even relatives. In return, they had eventually left him alone. That trivial conversation had been his first break with solitude in years, and he had enjoyed it.

Jerry began to take inventory of his life. In his own mind, his handicap and his bankbook made him the most worthless person on earth. In all his life, he had never had more than $365 a month, and that was from Social Security. He was 19 years old, he had absolutely no money, he was uneducated, crippled, and he didn't have a friend in the world. He had nothing. He had nothing to lose.

Jerry studied Zion Community Church from his window the following week. Going to Sunday services would require much planning. Mr. Bates' class started at 9:30, he remembered, and he figured he would need thirty minutes to walk the few blocks without working up a sweat. He prayed that they would accept him.

Precisely at 9:30, Jerry summoned up his courage and entered the room where Bates was teaching.

"Come in! I've been waiting for you," Bates said. "People, this is a friend of mine, Mr. Jerry Williamson, and he's new in town."

Thirty people turned toward the door and smiled a welcome, and Jerry wanted to run. But someone offered a chair, others introduced themselves, and Jerry was settled into the circle of people. He quickly became the center of attention.

"Where are you from?"

"What brought you to California?"

"Why, I live less than two blocks from you!"

He was fascinated at their interest. Jerry found himself talking like he did this every day. He began to relax. Within five minutes, he was even laughing.

Bates began the class with a prayer, and Jerry followed the motions of the crowd. Easy enough, he thought. Just watch everyone else and copy. He was more concerned about nodding at the proper intervals than listening to the lesson, but he heard the words and tried to pay attention. He was feeling pretty good about his success in this game.

Jerry can pinpoint the exact moment he began losing. Bates asked the group to follow along in their Bibles at a certain passage. Seeing that Jerry did not bring a Bible, the woman next to him held out hers to share. Up until this point, Jerry had nothing to lose. Now he could possibly lose the one ounce of pride he had left in front of the people he wanted most to impress. His palms began to sweat and his hand shook as he held on to the corner of the Bible. Jerry stared intently at the page while Bates read, and he prayed that it would be over soon.

At the end of the lesson, Jerry quickly gathered his crutches and said his goodbyes. The people in the class watched with concern as he left in such a hurry, but Jerry mistook their concern for condescending. He was ten years old again, and the whole world was laughing at him. He left the room in shame and hurried down the church steps.

Jerry was exhausted by the time he reached his house, but his panic had eased a bit, and he was thinking more clearly. He stared out the window toward the church. How stupid, he thought, for a man like me to try to mix with people like that. He thought about the experience for a long time, until finally, he was able to make peace with himself. They hadn't really laughed, he realized, but it was a close call. It had been stupid to take such a chance. He was not meant to be with people, he decided, and never again would he be so bold. He was content with the decision, and once again, Jerry resolved himself to a lonely, solitary life.

Because of that resolve, he was a little surprised to see Don Bates headed toward his house again, but he was ready with answers. Yes, Mr. Bates, he would say, I really enjoyed your service this morning. Very nice people. Yeah, maybe I'll stop by again sometime if I get the chance. Jerry planned to smile and very politely lie about going back. Mr. Bates and the whole group would forget him in a few days, and they would leave him alone.

As Bates ascended the steps to the porch, Jerry held the screen door open and began his act. But Bates did not ask if Jerry would come back. Instead, the two sat on the sofa once again and chatted about the weather, the city, the church. When Jerry eventually delivered his speech about what a fine lesson Bates had given, Bates just laughed a little and said he did his best.

"But you know," he said, "it's hard to stand up there in front of so many people and speak your mind.

I have to build up the courage all over again every week."

They sat in silence for a while, and Jerry thought how nice it was for this man to share with him something so personal. Others had tried to get Jerry to open up, but none had ever discussed themselves with him. Jerry was lost in his own thoughts when he noticed that Bates' expression had grown serious.

"I watched you during the lesson," Bates said. "There was one thing I felt I had to come over here and ask you about. I noticed that you seemed nervous when we started the Bible reading. I was just wondering if I said something at that time that bothered you."

Trying to bluff his way through, Jerry replied, "Nervous? No, I wasn't nervous. I guess I just felt a little funny when all those people got those Bibles out and started to read from them."

Without even hesitating, Bates said, "You know, from time to time people come to my class and because we read together, they get a little concerned. It is not unusual for someone to be sitting there who has trouble reading and they are afraid everyone may know that.

"Jerry, I was just wondering if that might have been your concern. Were you worried about the reading that we did this morning?"

Jerry sat frozen on the couch as he felt the impact of the words he had dreaded most in his life. He felt it in his gut, like a blow to the stomach, and the question echoed in his head. Jerry's illiteracy was more embarrassing to him than his physical handicap had ever been. He had moved to this place to get away from people who knew, and now, this man threatened his whole façade.

His mind raced back to his hometown. On every bus ride, he had held a book to his face. Sometimes at noon, he would sit on the steps of the city courthouse and pretend to read a newspaper. When crowds stopped to read advertisements posted in store fronts, he would stare at the words over someone's shoulder. If no one knows, no one can laugh, and he had spent years perfecting the image.

Jerry's first impulse was to scream at Bates, "Of course I can read! Do you think I'm an idiot?" and he jerked around on the couch to blurt out the denial.

But as Jerry looked up at the man sitting next to him, the words faltered. He saw the eyes and felt the sincerity in Bates' face as he watched Jerry struggle with an answer. His expression lacked contempt or mockery. Here was an educated, important man who cared about the life of Jerry Williamson. It was time to shoot straight. He looked his guest straight in the eye and said, "No, Mr. Bates. I can't read and I can't write, and yes sir, that bothered me this morning."

Jerry held his solemn gaze until he saw the tears begin to surface in Bates' eyes. Then he broke. He covered his face in his hands and began to sob, half out of relief and half from shame. The problem he had hidden all his life was out, but it didn't matter. The trust he felt from Bates was complete. Someone cared.

What began that night would turn out to be the hardest and most important task of Jerry's life. Bates and his wife would become his teachers in more ways than one. Bates had returned to Jerry's house that evening with his wife, who would teach him how to read and write.

Jerry was a remarkable student with a brilliant mind. And he had the determination and desire to push for an education. He received his GED within the year, and four years later graduated from college with a bachelor's degree in business.

More importantly, Jerry had learned his worth. Through the Bates' and the church, he had met people who would teach him the meaning of friendship. He found that he had something to offer, that people need not merely pity him. He learned to aim high, and he no longer thought of himself as worthless. Because of one man's invitation, this poor, crippled man had found himself.

Five years after his meeting with Don Bates, I sat with Jerry at the fund-raising banquet for Zion Community Church. More than 2,500 people filled the convention center where he had been asked to speak. The banquet was the last event of the fund-raising program, and the people had responded in mass. Jerry was one of three members who had been asked to share their testimonies of sacrifice. He had never addressed a small group—much less a crowd of this size—and he was nervous.

Personally, I was concerned. From my standpoint, Zion Community Church would not come close to reaching its potential as far as financial goals were concerned unless something dramatic happened. The missing link was that always elusive example of specific sacrifice. Although the first two testimonies were excellent, I still sensed that the concept of sacrifice had not been communicated. At this point, there was still no pattern for the people to follow.

But when two men lifted Jerry to the podium and he began to speak, I realized that God had something special in store for all of us.

Jerry stood at the podium and told 2,500 people his deepest secret—that until five years ago, he could not read or write. He told of his first visit to Zion Community Church, of his fear, of his humiliation, and of his decision never to go back. He talked about Don Bates and how he and his wife taught him self-respect, as well as to read and write.

"Most of you know my story from there," he said, "because every one of you have been a part of it. I graduated from college two weeks ago, and I'm doing maintenance work at the church until I can find a job in my field. All of that happened because one day Don Bates came to my house and invited me to this church.

"When I heard about the building program for our church, I wanted more than anything to be a part of it.

So I took inventory again, but this time, I took financial inventory. Before I began working at the church, the most I had ever made was $365 a month, and that was Social Security disability. As a maintenance man, I make almost $600 a month.

"Folks, I didn't know there was that much money in the world.

"I already tithe—that's about $60 a month. And I figure that on top of that, I can give $25 a month more. My gift to the church is $25 a month for the next three years. For me, that's $900. I can't believe I'm going to give that much!

"Last night, I told a friend of mine what I planned to do. He said, 'Jerry, $25 is a lot of money for a guy like you to give. Ain't it gonna hurt to give that money to the church?'"

Jerry paused in his speech and looked at the ground. Choking back tears, he finished.

"No," I told him. "It's not going to hurt. It's not going to hurt at all. You see, it never does hurt when you give to something you love."

Fourteen days later, the church held a Victory Service to announce the total commitments pledged to the building program. The total given was almost twice as much as had been projected.

Obviously, others learned a lesson from Jerry that night—nothing profound or deeply theological, just the simple lesson that "it never does hurt when you give to something that you really love."

▲ ▲ ▲

AN OBSERVATION

▼ ▼ ▼

When people are evaluating their giving they often return to thoughts of the blessings they have received from the church. In Jerry's case those blessings are counted in self-respect, self-image and the all-encompassing love of God.

But others have reflected on other blessings and from that reflection expressed their thanksgiving through sacrificial giving. A child reclaimed from drugs was the catalyst for the gift of a couple in Wyoming. Three children who made it to adulthood untouched by the ravages of inner city life created the reason for giving by a couple in Detroit. The stories are many.

Perhaps we should all ask ourselves what life would be like without the influence of the church and its community of believers. Where does the church stand on the priority of things important to us? Does our giving reflect that priority in our life?

Someone once said, "Sacrifice is taking from something you love in order to give to something you love more."

A very wealthy man once told me that he was giving $10,000 to the new sanctuary fund at the church.

In the course of the conversation, I had an opportunity to ask him how he had arrived at that decision. He replied, "I decided a long time ago that I would give $10,000 to anything."

How tragically sad. If only he could learn, if only we could all learn, that it never hurts to give to something you love.

CHAPTER XIV

THE JOB ON SATURDAY

When Barney Harris died, everyone came to the funeral. And that is the way it probably should have been because Barney had worked for the Baptist Convention for more than thirty years. As a young man, he had taken a position with the Convention to help build new Sunday Schools in churches across the state. After completing that task, he moved on to another and another and another, until a lifetime had been spent in service with the Convention.

Barney had travelled every backroad in the state as he carried out his duties over the years. He knew every McDonalds in the state and had spent more nights in hotel rooms than even he cared to remember. Once, as a gag gift at Christmas, his wife Norma gave him a robe with a Holiday Inn symbol embroidered on the front. Everyone in the family laughed, but the following month when his son fell on the ice and broke his arm and Barney was in the Holiday Inn in Huntsville and couldn't come home, the joke did not seem very funny. But that was his job. He was overworked and underpaid, and perhaps until the day he died, he was underappreciated.

One day, Barney was driving down a back county road going to visit a pastor of a church with fewer than fifty members when he suddenly felt the sharp pain of death approaching.   He pulled the car over to the side of the road, turned on his flashers, pushed the seat back, and right there, behind the wheel of the car that he had driven over 100,000 miles in the service of his Lord, he died.

He died on a country road.   A few days later, in a neighborhood church in the capital city, they had a funeral service for him.   There were lots of flowers, both real and verbal.   Yes, one day Barney Harris died and everybody came to the funeral.

People talked about what a great man he was and what a contribution he had made to the Lord's work. They talked about what a sacrifice he had made to go into this type of work, because everybody knew that denominational workers were underpaid.   Everybody talked about Barney as though he were a saint, and perhaps he was.   But after the funeral, everybody went home and forgot about the one person he loved more than his work, Norma Harris.

When Norma settled into the new life fate had given her, she realized things were going to change. She found that most of her friends were gone, all of her income from the Convention was gone, and the pension left by Barney after thirty years of faithful service was less than $500 a month.   She thought to herself that Barney was not the only one in the family to sacrifice for the Baptist Convention.   But being a realist, she accepted the facts.   For the first time in her life, she was going to have to look for a job.

Now, a lot of sixty-year-old women would have panicked at this point. But there are a few things you should know about Norma Harris. Norma was a fighter. Nevermind that she had never worked a day in her life outside her home. And nevermind that she had no marketable skills. Nevermind that she had only two years of college. Nevermind any of that.

Norma had a voice that could be heard across the state, all the aggressiveness of a kid out of college, and more determination than she probably needed. No one ever dared tell Norma that it couldn't be done.

Her first round of interviews could have been made into a TV sitcom. Everything possible went wrong. Her first interview was with one of the largest department stores in the city. The personnel director was a second year graduate from the state university and felt it her obligation to get Norma out of the job market rather than interview her for a prospective job.

"What was your last date of employment?"

"1953, when I sold magazines door-to-door when Barney was in college."

"What was your major in college—back then?"

"I didn't finish college, but I've read a lot over the years, if that helps."

It didn't!

"What kind of position do you think you are qualified to fill?"

"Probably none, but I'm a fast learner."

Now, multiply that interview about ten times, and you have Norma's introduction to the working world. The average person would have been completely disillusioned with the process. To that extent, Norma was perfectly normal. At wits-end, with money getting extremely tight, she finally caved in. The final blow came when a well-meaning friend came over one night and suggested that she just stop looking for a job and move in with her sister in Kansas City.

The suggestion itself was the final straw. This proud, independent woman just placed her head on the kitchen table and wept buckets of tears. Surely this wasn't the end of her life of self-sufficiency. With no further helpful suggestions, her friend went home leaving Norma to start the evaluation process all over again.

Step number one was to sell the house. She and Barney had bought it seven years before, and she probably had an equity in it of about $20,000. By selling most of her furniture, she could probably raise another $5,000. That being the first step, she proceeded to take it. While never once stopping the job search, the process of house selling was begun.

The first offer came from a "friend" of Barney's at the office. The offer was for $5,000 less than the appraised value. The second offer involved her carrying some of the financing and, of course, that was out of the question. On and on it went. The real estate agents worked hard, but nothing, absolutely nothing, happened.

During this time, there were three things that happened every day. First, Norma looked for a job. Second, she pushed to sell the house. And third, she came closer and closer to totally running out of money. At Barney's death, their total savings was less than $4,500. That, and a pension of $473.48 a month with a house payment of $355.75 a month, and any novice accountant could see the end in sight. As the professionals would say, "Given the current rate of outgo, Ms. Harris's financial resources were expected to diminish to zero within the next sixty days."

Things were not looking good.

And then it happened. Within the space of three days, she got an offer on the house and an offer of a job. Either one would have been a godsend. Together, they were almost too much to handle. A quick call to invite her two best friends over for dinner, a nice warm soak in a hot tub, and Norma was ready to tackle the world all over again.

First of all, the house sale. After all commissions and fees, she was able to net $17,900. A friend helped her to invest in a bank CD that paid 12 percent, so she now had added $179 per month to her income. Things were looking up!

The job offer was the best part. A local bookstore was opening in the mall on her side of town, and she had gotten a job as a sales clerk working five days a week from 9:00 a.m. to 6:00 p.m. The pay was $4.75 per hour. On a forty-hour week, she would gross $190 and take home $162 each pay day. Not spectacular, but a lot better than she had the week before.

After the sale of the house, she moved into an apartment, $375 per month, bills paid, and settled in for the day-to-day job of living. She had a job income of almost $729 a month, savings income of $179 a month, and don't forget Barney's pension after thirty years of service of $473.48. Total income before taxes was $1,381.48. As Norma put it, "Not much, but by crackey, it's mine. I'm going to make it."

And she did! Within a few months, Norma had adjusted to the life she had, and everything was back to normal. Her life revolved around three basic activities: her job, her church, and what she called "her hobby."

As far as the job was concerned, the manager of the bookstore only wished that he could clone Norma. She had to be the hardest worker he had ever seen. She came early and worked late. She covered at night for the younger girls who needed time off for that important date. She sold books and arranged titles. She worked stock and kept inventory. Because she had never had a job, she was determined to do this one right.

So, five days a week, eight hours a day, the bookstore reaped the benefits of all the determination and drive that Norma had to offer. Her manager complimented her dedication endlessly, but Norma thought that was nonsense. She had decided to do a good job; therefore, she was doing it. "For heaven's sake," she would say, "what is all the fuss about?"

As far as church was concerned, it absolutely filled her every free moment. Having had no children of her own, Norma had adopted the entire congregation at Northway Baptist as her own. For thirty-three years she had taught in the children's department. She had taught the parents of the present six-year-old children's class, and certainly no grandmother ever felt such pride in her very own grandchildren.

The same energy given to her job was duplicated with the children at church. She put fresh flowers in the department every weekend. Years and years ago, she and Barney had started that weekly tradition, and now, even with the added burden of doing it alone, she continued the process. Wednesday evening teacher training sessions, Thursday visitation, week-long preparation for teaching times, phone calls to parents and children—all of these were as much a part of her weekly routine as was catching the bus each weekday and going to work.

Now on top of all of this, she had her "hobby." Her hobby was a weekly visit to the neighborhood nursing home. She brought a ray of sunshine to those elderly people who, having once been a part of the church, now were unable to attend. Remember that voice I mentioned before? That was the voice that even the hardest of hearing could understand. That voice led in the singing, told jokes to the "girls," said sweet things to the men, and generally brought joy and happiness to everyone there.

Every Tuesday night immediately following work, she was there. If it rained, she came wet. If it snowed, she came cold. She always came. Sometimes she brought others with her, only to see them grow tired of the weariness of it all. The next week, she would come alone. But every week she came. Her "hobby" was the brightest moment in the lives of everyone at the home.

Job, church, and her hobby. And some say there is nothing to keep them busy. They should follow Norma Harris around for a day or two. Energy seemed to abound in the atmosphere for her, and she reached up and accepted her share only to give it back to others in return.

When Northway went into the stewardship program to raise funds for the new children's building, there was a special training meeting scheduled for teachers. At that meeting, Norma and the other one hundred plus teachers in the Sunday School organization heard the pastor make a special appeal for their teaching support.

He said, "Next Sunday, I am going to lay the groundwork for our people to begin the decision process related to finding God's will in this matter of giving. I am going to ask that, as you prepare your lessons for this Sunday, you give special attention to the concept of sacrifice. Every person in our church will need to come to grips with that concept if the new children's building is to be a reality. "

With that introduction, he then taught a very deep and theologically sound lesson on giving. The desired result would be the teachers returning to their classes to present the same type of lesson. Perhaps all of that is well and good if you are teaching adults, but how do you explain the concepts of "giving and sacrifice" to a group of six-year-old children? Certainly, that is not an easy task.

Norma found, as she prepared to develop the concept for the six-year-old level, that a lot of adults, including herself, had never come to grips with the concept of sacrifice. The next Sunday as she brought the lesson time to the children and as she explained in elementary terms these concepts, it became clear that Norma was teaching Norma as much as the children.

The children talked about what God had given them and what they would give back to Him. Maybe the children never did understand the philosophical definitions of giving, but Norma did. Somewhere in the middle of the story lesson time, she decided that she would be a part of the building program.

For the next few days, she struggled with her decision. When she told a few of her friends that she wanted to be a part of the building program, almost all of them tried to talk her out of it. They felt that at sixty-two years of age, it was time for her to take it easy. Often they would say, "You and Barney have sacrificed so much for the church. Now it's time for someone else to carry the load."

They were kind and well-meaning. They simply did not know the depth of Norma's resolve. She was not about to change her mind. How do you teach the children about giving if you do not give? How do you talk about sacrifice if you do not sacrifice? In Norma's value system, there was simply no question that she had to be a part. Quite frankly, she was not concerned with the sacrifices of Barney over the years gone by. His sacrifices had little to do with her at this time in her life. And although she understood that the intentions of her friends were good, she felt that it really was not any of their business either. Norma was going to experience personal sacrifice at this point in her life, and the results of that sacrifice would be between herself and God.

In order to make the "right" decision, Norma went through a process of studying her priorities. She worked a job to make a living. She gave a great deal of time to teach at the church—that paid nothing in money. Certainly, her "hobby" paid nothing. Actually, those three things consumed her life.

Since the job was the only moneymaker for her, she put that part of her life under the microscope. She worked five days a week, eight hours a day. But somehow she knew that if she was going to be a part of the building program, it would only be possible as a result of her job. After a lot of prayer and a lot of soul-searching, she picked up the phone and called her supervisor. An appointment was set for the next morning.

"Norma, you can't be serious!" were the first words out of the supervisor's mouth.

She explained in more detail.

"Norma, this is crazy. You can't be serious!" Sounds of a broken record.

But Norma was serious. She wanted a job on Saturday. She wanted to work eight more hours a week. No, she didn't need it to live on. No, she wasn't under a financial burden. No, she didn't need a loan. What she needed was a job on Saturday and she wanted it right here in the bookstore.

When her supervisor finally decided that it was useless to argue, he gave in and gave her an additional eight hours on Saturday. How did that translate into commitment? The next Sunday, Norma brought her commitment card by the church office. Her commitment was for $5,280. Exactly the amount of her additional after-tax income.

▲ ▲ ▲
AN OBSERVATION
▼ ▼ ▼

Again we return to a story of one who shared a specific dollar amount in her testimony. Often I am asked whether or not we encourage people to share the dollar amount of their commitment. Certainly, we realize that is a personal decision and must be made by the individual, but the fact is the sharing of dollar amounts can have a significant effect on the result of a program.

Let me explain. Norma Harris (not her real name) was a member of the church where I am a member. Our company has, over the years, conducted two programs for this church. We were attempting to raise a significant amount of money in the second program, and frankly, as a professional in this field, I was not totally convinced that our goals were within reach.

As we moved into the final weeks, I was certain that they were not. We had encouraged the people to begin the decision process in their lives and see what God would do with them. It was a good idea, but here in the final days, nothing was happening.

On the second Sunday of our intensive promotional time, Norma Harris was asked to give her testimony. Everyone in the church knew Norma and knew of her struggles since Barney's death. On that Sunday, she stood before the congregation and shared her story. She told of the period of time after Barney had died and of her fear of having no income.

She openly shared her preparation to teach her six-year-olds and how the preparation of the lesson that week had literally changed her concept of sacrifice. She told of her well-meaning friends and of her supervisor who had thought her a little crazy for going to work an extra day in order to be able to give. And then she told of her commitment.

"As a result of this learning pilgrimage, I am going to be able to give $5,280 to the program for our new children's building. I feel that, for me, at this point in my life, that is almost a miracle. I want you to know that when I got serious about this business of sacrifice, God opened the doors for me to walk through."

On Tuesday after that testimony on Sunday, George Thomas, an attorney in our church who sat on the personnel committee with me, called my office and suggested lunch the next day. Over the salad, I sensed that George was struggling with something. Finally, he got to the point.

"For three weeks, I have looked for an answer to this business of giving," he began. "Sunday when I came to the service, I had come prepared to turn in my commitment. It was going to be $10,000. Then Norma told her story.

"Ben, I paid over $10,000 for a new boat last year. I was about to say that my church and its needs were right up there with my recreational needs. Wow! How shallow I have been.

"If Norma Harris can give over $5,000, then it's time for me to get serious about this thing. I have a piece of property that's worth about $150,000. Let's look at some ways for me to give it. I had planned to build a home on it. It's out by the golf course, but somehow after hearing Norma, I just feel that this is a step I need to take."

Now I ask you. What if Norma had given a testimony and at the end had said, "Oh yes, I believe in this project so I am going to give a sacrificial commitment. "

What if that had been the way it had ended? All of us who heard her would have filtered her testimony through our own process and come up with an estimate. I might have said that she would have been one of the faithful ones like so many I have seen give a dollar per week—$156 over three years. George Thomas might have said that $300 sounded about right.

But, no. Norma did not allow us that luxury. Not boastfully and not braggingly, she just said, "This is what I am doing and this is how I made my decision. " All at once, I, along with 1,200 other members of our church, knew that Norma was serious. We also knew the standard of sacrifice had been set for the rest of us.

What was the worth of Norma's gift? Was it the $5,280 she would personally give or was it the $140,000 increase in George Thomas's gift that came as a result of her testimony? I do not know the answer to that question, but this I do know. George Thomas, and, if I am honest, Ben Gill, would not have been as serious about their decision process had it not been for Norma's openness and her sharing a $5,280 commitment.

Over the years, we have led hundreds of programs where people chose not to give dollar testimonies. Certainly that is a personal choice, and as a consulting firm we would be remiss if we tried to dictate that decision.   However, while it is not my place to tell people that they must share the dollar amount when giving their testimony, it is my place to point out that the end result may be dramatically different if they do.

Somehow people always fear that dollar amount testimonies will be seen as bragging. That simply is not a fact of reality. It is not easy to stand before a congregation and lay bare the steps of discovery related to finding and ultimately doing God's will. It is not easy, but I have come to feel in my own life that God's blessings are rather specific. Perhaps He can use my specific testimony to influence others. If so, then I can do no less.

CHAPTER XV

THE OIL WELL

S ome years ago our firm was involved in a major church fund-raising project in Tennessee. I had sold the program, and several months into the program I had gone back to speak at the Advance Commitment dinners. I had been with the pastor and the field consultant the day before as we checked on every area of the program. A late snack, a look at the 10:00 p.m. news, and off to sleep. I was scheduled for one more day on-site that would end with one final dinner that evening.

Somehow I just knew that this particular day was going to be an interesting one. It started with my phone ringing at 4:00 a.m. with some fellow trying to locate his girlfriend. That little event was followed by the room service waiter knocking on my door at 6:30 a.m. with a wonderful meal of bacon and eggs. The only problem was I had not ordered any bacon and eggs. So as I say, this day just had to be an interesting one with that kind of beginning.

As the day progressed, I found myself working on a multitude of things that would normally have been handled by our field consultant. The promotion committee was having problems, the banquet chairman was having difficulty with the convention center, the pastor had decided to be out of town the day of the Victory Service, and on and on it went. Before the afternoon had passed, I was completely convinced that our program field consultants were underpaid and overworked.

Finally, about 4:00 in the afternoon I received a call from the pastor. Normally he would have picked me up at the hotel for the Advance Commitment dinner, but tonight he had made arrangements for Joe and Bev Timberly to drop by and take me to the dinner site.

As I hung up the phone, I was a little more than perturbed. I had planned to spend the travel time with the pastor that evening going over some areas of the program that needed his personal attention. A long time ago I learned that if a program is to be successful, there are just some things that the pastor must attend to personally. This was going to be my opportunity to discuss those items with him.

But, nevertheless, this was not to be the night for that discussion. It seemed I would have to stay over the following morning for that. This would throw my entire schedule off for the week, but in my opinion, I had no choice. It was a little frustrating to learn later that the pastor had changed plans because he wanted to give his dog a bath. It is always ego-deflating to come in second to a dog—and an ugly one, at that.

As I looked over the committee list, it dawned on me that I did not know the Timberlys. They had been invited to the Advance Commitment dinner, but I simply could not get faces with the names. I never like to be totally in the dark. So I called Ben Harris, the campaign chairman, and asked him to tell me about them.

I knew I was in trouble when Ben began to laugh. He informed me that I would really like Joe. As he said, "Gill, you will never have to say even one word. By the time you get over the thirty-minute ride to the dinner, you will know everything there is to know about Joe. He will tell you about his family, his business, his car, and his sex life. Friend, good luck and God bless!"

Ben Harris had understated the case. But before I give you the gory details, let me tell you a little about this particular church.

I had been called to St. Mark's church in Memphis about six months earlier to discuss the possibility of raising money for a new educational wing. The moment I stepped on the church property, I knew that I had one major problem—I was about fifty years late.

The sanctuary was a rather modern building from the 1970's, but the educational part of the facility had not so much as seen a paint brush in over thirty years. Looking at the front of the building, I counted fourteen windows either broken or completely covered with plywood. The steps that led up to the entrance were narrow, and the concrete was cracked and broken in several places. The metal railing bowed in the middle from generations of playful children who had no doubt used it for the Sunday morning slide. All in all, the building was a hopeless disaster from a physical viewpoint. I soon discovered that it was not much better from the spiritual perspective.

When I entered the building, I found myself in a narrow hallway with dim lighting and bland, colorless walls. When I entered the committee room, I found a committee that, in many ways, matched their surroundings. There was a sense of pessimism and despair. They were not expecting to accomplish anything and they were well on their way to succeeding.

When the committee voted on the project, the vote was divided. Four members felt a new educational building was a must if the church was ever to regain a position of progressive ministry. Three members felt religious educational training was best left up to the family. As they said, "You don't read anywhere in the Bible about educational buildings."

The process was slow, but over a period of time, the thinking of the committee became a bit more progressive. After five long months and countless meetings, they decided to go to the congregation and recommend an educational building. They also recommended that the church employ our firm to assist in the fund-raising project. To the surprise of all of us, the vote was 489 to 7 in favor of the project.

From the overwhelming positive nature of the vote, it was evident that the committee was far from representative of the church.

I tell you all of this because I later learned that one of the seven negative votes came from my soon to be host for the evening, Joe Timberly. If I had known all of the facts on this particular day, I would have considered taking a taxi to the dinner.

From the moment I got in the car, Joe talked. He not only talked, he preached! First of all, he told me his opinion of people in my business. Of course, he said it jokingly, but Joe had a way of making his jokes in a very malicious manner.

He then told me of his philosophy of church growth, and his feelings about building educational facilities in particular. From his point of view, Christian education was an old-fashioned approach to be discarded in this modern world.

In a conversation with the pastor a few days later, I was told that Joe's frustration came from a bad experience he had in Sunday School when he was eleven years old. Isn't it strange how sometimes we carry deadweight around for years without even knowing it is there.

Then Joe moved to a subject that was dear to his heart. That subject dealt with his well-developed philosophy in the area of husband and wife relationships. In a nutshell, it was a very simple concept: keep them barefoot and pregnant and whatever you do—never allow them to think.

I know that there are a lot of men who hold to that way of thinking, but somehow I just did not expect it from a 36-year-old attorney who had a lovely University of Maryland-educated wife. But expect it or not, I knew that before the ride was over, I was going to get the whole story.

Here was a man who openly boasted that in ten years of marriage, he had never allowed his wife to be a part of any family decision. In fact, he reached the peak of boastfulness when he related the story about the purchase of their new home. "Yes, sir, Gill. I just went out one day and bought a house that I liked and picked up the phone and called Bev and told her to pack up. We were moving!"

What I really enjoyed was the way that Joe would stop after each of these little stories and say, "Now, isn't that right, Bev?" She always answered with a meek, "Yes, dear." This was becoming an interesting ride.

The real high point of the ride came when we drove by one of the largest banks in town. As we approached the bank, Joe pulled over to the curb, rolled down his window and stopped the engine. This was going to be an important story to him.

"Ben," he said, with a great deal of dramatic pause, "you see that bank over there?"

I would have had to have been absolutely blind to have missed it.

"I started that bank almost six years ago and it is now one of the largest in the city. I serve on the

Board. I am on the loan committee. And right at this very moment, I have over $500,000 cash sitting in that bank right there making money for me!"

That last statement surprised me. Most people do not want me to know how much money they have in the bank. I have always felt that most people think that if I know how much money they have, I may pressure them into giving it all away.

He continued, "Now, Ben. This is going to surprise you."

Yes. I could hardly wait!

"With all of the pull that I have in that bank, and with all of the money that I have in there, my little wife here can't write a check for one single cent. In fact, since the day we got married and I took over things, this little lady has not had her hands on one thin dime that didn't pass through my hands first. Most people wouldn't like it that way, but we get along just fine with this system. Don't we, Bev?"

I could see that Bev, his little wife, the little lady, was just bubbling over with enthusiasm.

With the speech finally ended, he started the car and drove on to the dinner. Imagine, if you can, the next fifteen minutes. Every moment, every second is filled with the sound of Joe's voice. On and on it goes from subject to subject. It is difficult to really put into words how long fifteen minutes can be under those circumstances.

At last we drove into the driveway of the home where our dinner was to be held. I couldn't get out of the car fast enough. Frankly, what I really wanted to do was go in and take a shower and wash Joe off.

As a casual observer, I watched Bev as she walked, ate, talked, and breathed in the shadow of Joe throughout the rest of the evening. It was an interesting study. I have learned over the years to not be critical of someone in that type situation, because one really never knows what they must go through when they are alone with the Joes of this world. But that evening, I saw a lovely, intelligent woman whose total being seemed to be negated by her husband. It was not a pleasant sight.

The purpose of the evening was to bring together a group of people whose commitment and dedication to the church were not in question, and ask them to make the first gifts to the program. We would then use their gifts as an encouragement to others who might be considering making a sacrificial commitment.

The usual format for the evening calls for the pastor to first speak to the need. I would then talk about sacrificial giving and ways that people often enhance their giving through commitments of tangible assets other than cash.

That evening, the pastor did a masterful job. He talked about the years of planning that had brought the church to this point in its history. He talked about ministry, and the way the new educational building would enhance the total work of the church. He talked about the commitment that he was seeing on the part of hundreds who had already worked in the program. It was as though everything that he said that night was inspired by God.

By the time I was introduced to share my part on the program, the people were ready to listen. They were eager to find out how it could all be done. With the pastor's excellent foundation, I was able to build on the ways of sacrifice. I used illustrations from other churches and underscored these illustrations with biblical examples. Every word seemed to flow as the message of giving was presented, and the people heard and were challenged. Only one who has experienced that kind of inner leadership can ever image the intense feeling that something unusual is about to happen.

I watched the people very closely as I spoke to the crowd. I was especially impressed that Bev seemed to be listening to every word. When I said that giving was a personal thing that no one could ever do for someone else, I could see that she was visibly moved. Others in the audience seemed to be touched by the message, but not to the depth that I saw written on Bev's face.

Finally, my part was over. At that point, Perry and Susan Hartman stood to tell the people of their experience in making their decision to give. They talked about the hours they had spent together seeking to know the right thing to do about their commitment. As they talked, I watched the people as they began to identify with Perry and Susan. Couple after couple

reached out to hold hands with their spouse as together
they shared the experience of the Hartmans.

Looking over the group, I saw two people who
were decidedly different from all the rest. Joe
Timberly was looking defiant. Bev Timberly was
looking inward. In that moment, it was obvious to me
that they were not a couple in this together, but rather
two separate and lonely individuals. It was a disturbing
observation from my vantage point.

It is customary after such a meeting for the people
to stand around and visit for a few minutes after the
formal meeting is over. This night the usual pattern
was being followed. The people were laughing and
visiting. True to form, Joe was the loudest of all.

I had been to the kitchen for a drink of water and
had started towards the living room, when I looked in
the hallway. There stood Bev trying to get my
attention. As I walked toward her, I could see that she
was extremely nervous.

With no preliminary statements, she blurted out,
"Ben, I want to give an oil well!"

Now I have seen Texas oil men give oil wells, but
never have I seen a housewife give one—especially a
housewife with the kind of profile I had seen from Bev.

Suddenly, she began to talk. She shared with me
that six years before Joe had bought a share in an oil
well in Oklahoma. In a moment of unusual generosity,
he had put the ownership interest in her name and had

told her that the income from it could be used any way she wanted to use it.

Almost apologetically she said, "Ben, there was a time when Joe was so generous. I know that he doesn't seem to be anymore, but he was once the kindest and most generous person you would ever want to meet. I have no idea whether he will give to this program, but even it he does, I know it will have nothing to do with me.

"For the past six years, I have put money aside from the oil well. Right now, I have over $11,000 that Joe doesn't know about. I had planned to start a business for myself, one that would be all mine, but after tonight, I want to give it to help build our new educational building."

How do you evaluate a gift like this one? Was it the sacrifice of seeing a dream vanish? Was it the sacrifice of seeing some sense of freedom fade? I really don't know.

The only thing I do know for sure is that the next Sunday, there was a check in the amount of $11,876 in the morning offering designated for the new building.

And, just as a footnote, you might be interested to know that the check was drawn on a bank not owned by Joe and the check was signed by Bev.

▲ ▲ ▲
AN OBSERVATION
▼ ▼ ▼

Bev was one of the quiet people whom I have known through the years. These are the people who just always seem to do the right thing at the right time with no desire for accolades. And the exciting thing to know is their numbers are legion.

They serve in every church, quietly going about their work for the Kingdom. And every congregation and every individual who knows such a person is better for it.

CHAPTER XVI

THE ONLY THING
THAT REALLY MATTERS

This is the second of only two stories in this series where the names have not been changed. In this one, the names have not been changed to protect the innocent. The event really happened just as I am about to share it with you. I was there and felt the impact of the moment in a very personal way.

Some time ago, we were contacted by Dr. Jasper Williams, pastor of Salem Baptist Church in Atlanta, Georgia, to discuss the possibility of our working with that church. Salem Baptist Church is one of the largest Afro-American congregations in the United States. Dr. Williams has been the pastor for almost twenty years, having gone there as Senior Pastor at the age of nineteen.

From the moment I met this man, I liked him. He was honest, forthright, and told it exactly like it was. The church had financial needs that were not being met. They had an opportunity to make an economic impact on their community, but needed money to do it. They had a need for youth educational programs, but no funds to implement them. They needed to renovate buildings and upgrade facilities.

Yes, in a few words, they needed money and needed it badly.

According to Pastor Williams, they had tried the gimmicks. They had tried emotion. They had tried guilt. None of those approaches had made a lasting impact on either the financial needs of the church or the lives of the people. They were looking to us for something different. That was a great responsibility, and we as an organization felt the weight of it.

After a few meetings to get to know one another, we accepted the challenge to conduct a major stewardship program for the church. We assigned a consultant to the program who had experience in inner city work. Knowing the job would be a big one, we rolled up our sleeves and went to work.

From the beginning, the program was a total joy for our staff. No pastor where we have worked has ever been more supportive of the ministry and staff of RSI than was Dr. Williams. Once each month, we bring our total staff from all over the United States and Canada to Dallas for a two-day meeting. For months, the highlight of our monthly meeting was the report that was brought from Salem Baptist Church.

We struggled with their problems. We rejoiced with their victories. We implemented new approaches to meet their specific needs, and we reworked old standby approaches in order to make certain that every base was covered. With every suggestion we made, Dr. Williams would simply say, "Well, brothers, you're supposed to know what you're doing—you tell us and we will do it. "

So we offered advice, and they followed that advice exactly as presented. Working with Salem Baptist Church and Dr. Jasper Williams was a consultant's dream!

In most of our programs, we move toward a final big event. Occasionally, that event is a banquet at a location away from the church. I have been in banquets where the expected attendance was less than a hundred, and others where multiplied thousands came together. But I have never been to one that was not later described as "one of the greatest nights in the history of the church. " It is simply always a wonderful evening.

As the church searched for a place in Atlanta to hold such an event, they soon realized that their options were few. Salem is a large church, and to find a room large enough to seat and feed the total congregation at one time was certainly a challenge. Finally, the Grand Ballroom at the downtown Marriott Marquis Hotel in Atlanta was reserved. The date was set and the program started moving toward that evening.

Over the years, I have tried to make it a practice not to attend the banquets. In my opinion, this is the church family coming together and an outsider can only be a distraction. Our consultants may attend the banquet, but even then, their role is to work in the background seeing that all of the wheels are turning. Because of that, I was surprised when our consultant suggested that I attend the Salem banquet.

"Ben," he said, "you just have to be there. This is going to be one of the greatest nights in history and you won't want to miss it!"

Thinking that he might be a bit prone to overstatement, I hesitantly booked a flight to Atlanta that would get me there in time to visit with Dr. Williams and share in the evening banquet with the congregation. How glad I was that I made that decision.

I sensed the electricity of the evening from the moment I walked into the ballroom. People were visiting and laughing with one another. Everyone was dressed in their finest. The people from the church who were working on the banquet had done an excellent job. Every "i" was dotted and every "t" crossed. There was to be a fifteen-minute video presented, and the two-story tall screens in both ends of the ballroom were beginning to draw a lot of attention. Truly, everyone was expecting something dramatic to happen.

At exactly 6:00 p.m., the meal service began. Dr. Williams had insisted that I sit with him at the head table. So much for working in the background. From there, I had a perfect view of the thousands of people now being served. Something was wrong. I could not put my finger on it, but something was out of place.

Turning to say something to our consultant, I glanced behind the speaker's table and saw stacks and stacks of information packets containing the commitment cards the people would be filling out later. They were sitting in huge boxes behind our table. The

one thing that had been overlooked was the fact that
these packets were supposed to be on the tables in easy
reach of the people when we came to the time for
commitment.

For about three minutes, we searched for a
solution. We realized that to get these to the individual
tables would require hundreds of people and precious
moments of time. We had a table hostess at each table
of ten people, but we hated to break into the program
and take thirty minutes to get the job done. We had no
choice. That was the best idea we could come up with
at the time.

Turning to Dr. Williams, I explained the situation
and started into our solution of the problem when he
stopped me. Very quietly he said, "I understand the
problem. Let me handle it." Then he simply took
another bite of steak and commented on how nice
everyone looked.

I am convinced that there are times when God
must wink to the angels and say, "Look at ol' Gill. He
doesn't know that I have this all worked out. He just
doesn't know all the items that I want on the agenda
tonight."

What happened next was so obviously of God that
it could not have been programmed or planned. As the
meal ended and after the planned program had been
completed, Dr. Williams walked to the speaker's stand.
When the crowd became quiet, he simply asked the
table hostesses to come forward. In about five minutes,

over two hundred hostesses were standing in lines waiting for his instructions.

And then, in a quiet voice, he began to talk to the people. As he talked, he began handing each hostess packets of material to take back to her table, one packet for each person there. He talked and distributed packets. He was doing in a smooth, quiet way what could have been very disruptive. It was not.

"Almost twenty years ago, you allowed me to become your pastor," he began. "I was nineteen years old. All of these years, we have been in this thing together."

The hostesses marched by.

"Over the years, we have seen our neighborhood taken over by other people. As a result of this program, we are going to start reclaiming our neighborhood. We have seen our young people ruin their lives with drugs and unwanted pregnancies. We are going to, as a result of this program, begin programs to combat the problems of our young people."

He slowly handed the hostesses the commitment packets and continued to talk.

"We're going to do this together. We're going to do it for our children and we're going to do it for ourselves and we are going to do it for the Lord."

By now, every eye is on him as he speaks. The crowd is totally silent as he continues.

"Some people say that this program is only for the rich. Some people say it is for the pastor. Some say it won't work, and others say that it is just a way to hustle money. But I say to them: 'This program is a chance for us to show who we are and what is important to us.'

"We talk about the church and what the church is going to do. I say it is time to look unto the Lord and ask ourselves the question, 'What am I going to do?'

"What I've done in the past isn't going to count. It's what I do right now that is going to tell me and tell others and tell the Lord where my heart is."

The packets were almost distributed. I sensed that he was coming to his close. I knew he was speaking from his heart, prepared for this moment only by his love for these people whom God had given him to shepherd.

"You know, someday I am going to die. Whether I am rich or poor makes no difference. Someday, I am going to die. After I die, my wife is going to go down to the tombstone store and she is going to order a stone to put on my grave.

"She is going to say to the stonecutter, 'This stone is for my husband, Jasper Williams, so I want you to chisel on the stone: Here lies Jasper Williams. August 12, 1941, dash, and then the date of my death.'

"Oh, my people, my children. Don't you know that the only thing that makes any difference is what I've done with the dash."

With that, he sat down.

The program went forward, and before we knew it, the evening was over. A lot of money was committed that night, and within a week the people had pledged more money than any inner city church in recent history. The program was a success from every angle.

As I got on a plane the next day and returned to Dallas, I could not help but think of the pastor's casual speech the night before. As I thought about it, everything about this ministry of giving suddenly came into perspective.

That's really all that giving is about. A person is born and then someday that person dies. The lives of most of us are spent receiving. From parents, friends, other associates—we take. They freely give, but we freely take as well.

But a few people take the model of others and integrate it into their own lives and learn to give. Those are the people I have shared with you. They are the happy people. They are the people who have found the joy of giving. They are the people who are doing something with the dash.

Sometime ago I visited with Bruce Larson, at that time Senior Minister of the University Presbyterian

Church in Seattle, Washington. Over lunch, he told me of a man he had once known who had been very successful financially. Then, at the age of sixty, it all started falling apart. His marriage broke up and his business failed. His children turned their backs on him and his friends even avoided social gatherings with him.

It was out of that bleakness he turned to the church. Out of that search, he found a personal relationship with God. A few days before our conversation, he sat with Dr. Larson and said, "You know, I never really thought I could be this happy. I don't have things anymore, but I have something else. All my life I spent taking. Now, at almost seventy, God has taught me how to give. I have never known such peace."

That's really it, isn't it? "Here lies Ben Gill, August 13, 1939, dash, whatever date I die." The only thing that really matters is what I did with the dash.

Now, after years and years of working with people in this ministry of Christian stewardship, I can only sum it up by reaffirming this fact. It has been my observation through the years that

THE HAPPIEST PEOPLE I KNOW
ARE THE PEOPLE
WHO HAVE COME TO KNOW
THE JOY OF GIVING.

ABOUT THE AUTHOR

Ben G. Gill is the acknowledged leader in the field of charitable fund-raising in America. As Founder and Chairman of Resource Services, Inc. (RSI) in Dallas, Texas, he leads an organization that raises hundreds of millions of dollars for charitable causes each year. Labelled "the biggest religious fund-raiser in America" by the *Dallas Morning News*, Gill has expanded his personal talents by building the premier fund-raising organization of our day.

In the business community, Gill is a much sought-after speaker in the field of corporate management. His seminars on *Visionary Leadership* are held across the nation and attended by many of the giants of corporate America.

To communicate with Ben Gill, or for more information about the services of RSI, please contact:

Resource Services, Inc.
12770 Merit Drive #900
Dallas, Texas 75251
800-527-6824